JOY!

Growing Strong Throughout Your Seasons of Life as a Teacher and Leader

Timothy D. Kanold

Foreword by Anthony Muhammad

Solution Tree | Press

Copyright © 2025 by Solution Tree Press

All rights reserved, including the right of reproduction of this book in whole or in part in any form.

555 North Morton Street
Bloomington, IN 47404
800.733.6786 (toll free) / 812.336.7700
FAX: 812.336.7790

email: info@SolutionTree.com
SolutionTree.com

Visit **go.SolutionTree.com/JOY** to access materials related to this book.

Printed in the United States of America

Library of Congress Cataloging-in-Publication Data

Names: Kanold, Timothy D., author.
Title: Joy! : growing strong throughout your seasons of life as a teacher
   and leader / Timothy D. Kanold.
Description: Bloomington, IN : Solution Tree Press, 2025. | Includes
   bibliographical references and index.
Identifiers: LCCN 2024040165 (print) | LCCN 2024040166 (ebook) | ISBN
   9781962188951 (paperback) | ISBN 9781962188968 (ebook)
Subjects: LCSH: Teachers--Job satisfaction. | Teachers--Mental health. |
   Reflective teaching. | Work-life balance.
Classification: LCC LB2840 .K343 2025 (print) | LCC LB2840 (ebook) | DDC
   371.1001/9--dc23/eng/20241211
LC record available at https://lccn.loc.gov/2024040165
LC ebook record available at https://lccn.loc.gov/2024040166

Solution Tree
Jeffrey C. Jones, CEO
Edmund M. Ackerman, President

Solution Tree Press
President and Publisher: Douglas M. Rife
Associate Publishers: Todd Brakke and Kendra Slayton
Editorial Director: Laurel Hecker
Art Director: Rian Anderson
Copy Chief: Jessi Finn
Senior Production Editor: Christine Hood
Copy Editor: Jessica Starr
Proofreader: Sarah Ludwig
Text and Cover Designer: Laura Cox
Acquisitions Editors: Carol Collins and Hilary Goff
Content Development Specialist: Amy Rubenstein
Associate Editors: Sarah Ludwig and Elijah Oates
Editorial Assistant: Madison Chartier

*To Abby, Maguire, and Wells: May you grow strong
in your seasons of life.*

May your journey be filled with JOY!

Visit **go.SolutionTree.com/JOY** to
access materials related to this book.

Table of Contents

About the Author ix
Foreword xi
Introduction 1

♥ **PART 1: FALL—A SEASON TO RENEW** **5**
    CHAPTER 1   Beginnings 7
    CHAPTER 2   Remember 11
    CHAPTER 3   Simple Joy 15
    CHAPTER 4   Breathe 19
    CHAPTER 5   Nature 23
    CHAPTER 6   Music 27
    CHAPTER 7   Yearning 31
    CHAPTER 8   Relationships 35
    CHAPTER 9   Habituation 39
    CHAPTER 10 Time 43
    CHAPTER 11 Hijacked 47
    CHAPTER 12 Perseverance 51
    CHAPTER 13 Thanksgiving 55
    Fall: A Season to Renew—Your Conclusions 59

♥ PART 2: WINTER—A SEASON TO BE RESOLUTE **61**

CHAPTER 1	Resolute 63
CHAPTER 2	Chronic Joy 67
CHAPTER 3	Silence 71
CHAPTER 4	Comparison 75
CHAPTER 5	Suffering 81
CHAPTER 6	Compassion 87
CHAPTER 7	Worry 91
CHAPTER 8	*Gezellig* 95
CHAPTER 9	Pause 99
CHAPTER 10	Balance 103
CHAPTER 11	Midlife 109
CHAPTER 12	Reflection 113
CHAPTER 13	Show 117

Winter: A Season to Be Resolute—Your Conclusions 119

♥ PART 3: SPRING—A SEASON TO SHOW RESOLVE **121**

CHAPTER 1	Finishing 123
CHAPTER 2	Acknowledging Joy 127
CHAPTER 3	Credibility 131
CHAPTER 4	Preparation 135
CHAPTER 5	Engagement 139
CHAPTER 6	Kindness 143
CHAPTER 7	Regrets 147
CHAPTER 8	*Zotheka* 151
CHAPTER 9	*Commuovere* 155
CHAPTER 10	*Meraki* 159
CHAPTER 11	Valedictory 163
CHAPTER 12	*Ubuntu* 167
CHAPTER 13	*Vanaprastha* 171

Spring: A Season to Show Resolve—Your Conclusions 173

- **PART 4: SUMMER—A SEASON TO REJUVENATE** **175**
  - CHAPTER 1   Rest 177
  - CHAPTER 2   Reminisce 181
  - CHAPTER 3   *Boketto* 185
  - CHAPTER 4   Vacation 189
  - CHAPTER 5   Friendship 193
  - CHAPTER 6   *Naz* 197
  - CHAPTER 7   Stretch 201
  - CHAPTER 8   Gratitude 205
  - CHAPTER 9   Purpose 209
  - CHAPTER 10   *Resfeber* 213
  - CHAPTER 11   Truth 217
  - Summer: A Season to Rejuvenate—Your Conclusions 219
- Afterword 221
- Acknowledgments 223
- Notes 227
- Index 237
- Praise for *JOY!* 241

About the Author

Timothy D. Kanold, PhD, is an award-winning educator and author. He formerly served as director of mathematics and science and as superintendent of Adlai E. Stevenson High School District 125, a model professional learning community (PLC) district in Lincolnshire, Illinois.

Dr. Kanold has authored or coauthored more than thirty-seven textbooks and professional development books on K–12 mathematics, school culture, and school leadership, including his best-selling and 2018 Independent Publisher Book Awards–winning book *HEART! Fully Forming Your Professional Life as a Teacher and Leader*. In 2021, he authored a sequel to *HEART!*, titled *SOUL! Fulfilling the Promise of Your Professional Life as a Teacher and Leader*. In addition, he coauthored the best-selling book *Educator Wellness: A Guide for Sustaining Physical, Mental, Emotional, and Social Well-Being* followed by *The Educator Wellness Plan Book and Journal: Continuous Growth for Each Season of Your Professional Life*.

Dr. Kanold received the 2017 Ross Taylor/Glenn Gilbert National Leadership Award from the National Council of Supervisors of Mathematics, the international 2010 Damen Award for outstanding contributions to education from Loyola University Chicago, the 1994 Outstanding School Administrator Award from the Illinois State Board of Education, and the 1986 Presidential Award for Excellence in Mathematics and Science Teaching.

Dr. Kanold is committed to equity, excellence, and social justice reform for the improved learning of students and school faculty, staff, and administrators. He conducts inspirational professional development seminars worldwide with a focus on improving student learning outcomes in mathematics through a commitment to the PLC process. He also teaches educators how to embrace chronic joy for a well-balanced, fully engaged professional life by practicing daily educator-wellness routines.

Dr. Kanold earned a bachelor's degree in mathematics education, a master's degree in applied mathematics from Illinois State University, and a master's degree in school psychology and administration from the University of Illinois. He received his doctorate in educational leadership and counseling psychology from Loyola University Chicago.

To learn more about Dr. Kanold's work, follow him @tkanold on X, @tkanold on Bluesky, and @tdkanold on Instagram.

To book Timothy D. Kanold for professional development, contact pdSolutionTree.com.

Foreword

by Anthony Muhammad

I met Dr. Timothy Kanold almost twenty years ago. The late Richard DuFour introduced us in the auditorium of Adlai E. Stevenson High School in Lincolnshire, Illinois. We exchanged pleasantries but did not form a relationship until 2012, when Dr. Kanold became a regular faculty member and presenter at the Professional Learning Communities at Work® (PLCs at Work) conferences headlined by Richard DuFour, Rebecca DuFour, and Robert Eaker. Dr. Kanold and I were breakout session presenters, members of the supporting cast. Though we worked in close proximity, our bond was not truly solidified until our mentor, Richard DuFour, was diagnosed with lung cancer in 2014, and eventually surrendered to the disease in 2017. Through the loss of a mutual dear friend and mentor, our friendship was truly formed.

Before knowing Dr. Kanold on a personal basis, I only knew him through his credentials, which are quite impressive. He was an accomplished mathematics teacher and leader, a superintendent of a national model school district, and a former president of the National Council of Teachers of Mathematics. I was a former social studies teacher who struggled in mathematics as a student, so I always viewed mathematicians and mathematics teachers as linear, logical, and stoic.

When Dr. Kanold and I truly formed our friendship, I quickly realized that his scope of excellence far exceeded my narrow stereotype of a "math guy." I found out that Dr. Kanold was as learned in matters of the heart as he was in mathematics. He proved this by writing two compelling books simply titled *HEART!*[1] and *SOUL!*[2] Both of these books have become staples in my library, and I have quoted them countless times in my books and presentations. Because of my affinity for these two wonderful books, I was very excited when I heard that Dr. Kanold was writing a third book, *JOY!*, as a companion to the previous books.

As Dr. Kanold was crafting the manuscript for this book in 2022, he and I attended a dinner with colleagues. While dining, he explained that he was working a new book titled *JOY!*, and he asked each one of us, "What does joy mean to you?" This seems, on the surface, like a pretty simple question. But as we explored the depth of this question, it was much more complex than it appeared. In my life, I have used the term *joy* on many occasions without analyzing its true meaning. I deeply contemplated my answer as the question circulated around the table. In my lifetime, I have experienced a lot of personal success, professional success, and financial success, but did those things really bring me joy?

As I formulated my response, I had an epiphany. Joy is a state of being—a safe place of peace. It is not what you've *done* or what you've *achieved*; it is part of who you *are*. So, when the question made its way around the table and it was my turn to answer, I thought about the word *authenticity*. As an African American Muslim author and educator, who has achieved international success and acclaim, I have had to give up a lot of my personal authenticity to achieve that success and acclaim. I have had to "code switch" and, at times, suppress my own authentic culture to influence, inspire, and motivate audiences, who typically have a different culture and worldview.

Over my thirty-four-year career, I have come to realize how much that sacrifice has done to my personal joy. Though I am grateful for the adoration and support of millions of educators who I have been blessed to help, this has made me happy but doesn't bring me joy. My professional life is *what I do*, but it is not *who I am*. So, when it was my turn to answer, I shared that joy, in my opinion, is to live authentically in my culture, language, and ethos—the space where I don't have to compromise *who I am* or *what I am* for others. This is what feeds my soul and gives me joy. Before this memorable conversation, I never considered what gave me joy, but that moment has enhanced my life ever since.

As educators navigate the disruption of a devastating global pandemic, students' increased social and emotional needs, teacher shortages, political turmoil, and budget cuts, I believe this book is necessary now more than ever. As they returned to the classroom full time in 2022, they discovered that teacher morale was at an all-time low.[3] The return was rocky, and they did not truly address the mental, physical, and emotional strain that two years of isolation, death, and fear had taken on both students and teachers. Not only were teachers struggling with morale and optimism, but both teachers and students set records for absenteeism.[4] If there was ever a time to publish a book for educators about *joy*, this is the time!

Dr. Kanold makes an important distinction about joy that I think is worth noting as you navigate this important book. He affirms that people often confuse the concepts of *joy* and *happiness* as synonymous, and they are not. He considers happiness as an experience that is subject to what is happening around you. He describes joy as something that happens within you—a constant state of being. With all that educators face today, a book that helps create an impenetrable sense of internal joy is worth its weight in gold.

I encourage you to address the research, ideas, and guidance presented in this book with an open mind. I am confident that every educator who has ever entered our profession began their journey with a heightened sense of optimism. This book will teach you that external conditions may sometimes compromise your happiness, but if you are firmly rooted in your authentic self, conditions can never take away your joy. I wish I had access to this book thirty-four years ago when I started my educational journey. I truly could have anchored myself in my own authenticity and transcended circumstances that seemed daunting, but were truly no match for a true, authentic self.

I believe that a careful and analytical review of this book can save some educators from early retirement, burnout, and hopelessness. It is true that you cannot be much good to others if you are no good to yourself. I tip my hat in salute to Dr. Kanold for writing this book, and I have deep respect for the reader who analyzes this book, applies its principles, and dares to become a better person and a better educator.

Introduction

Joy does not simply happen to us. We have to choose joy and keep choosing it every day.

—Henri J. M. Nouwen

Life is hard. Life is messy for everyone in different ways. Yet, life can be joyful too.

What makes your life a story of joy? What daily steps can you take to create and curate conditions for joy? Strategies for answering these questions is the purpose of this book.

The joy story of your professional and personal life unfolds one scene after another. One season after another. As those scenes and seasons cycle by—one school year after the next—the decisions you make about joy follow an arc that leaves an impact.

Joy can often feel elusive. Yet, we don't have to wait for a life of joy. We can choose it now!

For the purposes of this book, your *joy journey* is defined as a state of mind to be cultivated independent of your circumstances, including times of grief, stress, or uncertainty. Throughout the book, there are phrases such as *finding joy, bringing joy, acknowledging joy, simple joy, chronic joy, delayed joy, compelling joy, curating joy, sustaining joy,* and *cultivating joy*; together, we explore them all.

Joy and *happiness* are often used interchangeably, yet *joy* is different from *happiness*. Happiness is experiential and, therefore, comes and goes throughout the days, weeks, months, and seasons. Happiness is based on what is happening *around* us. Joy is based on what is happening *within* us. Joy, then, is an *internal* action, a daily decision to practice walking through life because of the good, and despite the difficult, circumstances we live within. Joy is a deliberate and intentional pursuit, season after season and school year after school year.

Joy shares space within other emotions—sadness, fear, anger, worry, suffering, compassion, tenderness, excitement, and more. Joy endures hardships and trials and connects us to our meaning and purpose. *Happiness can't.* Joy is more than a sensation. Joy is a pervasive and constant state of well-being that we cultivate and curate throughout our lives during times of grief or uncertainty. Thus, we can continuously sustain our joy journey independent of our circumstances. The chapters of this book provide a pathway toward sustained joy.

Research about neurotransmitters can inform your actions toward a sustained joy journey. There is a neuroscience, research-affirmed pathway that informs our daily growth toward joy, including neurotransmitters that promote positive feelings: dopamine, serotonin, oxytocin, and endorphins.[5] Brain research confirms that roughly 40 percent of your disposition toward joy is genetic, and the other 60 percent can be developed.[6]

The subtitle of this book, *Growing Strong Throughout Your Seasons of Life as a Teacher and Leader*, reveals the book's organizational structure. As educators, we chose a lifetime of work designed in yearly cycles, one school year after another. And each school year has a beginning season (fall), a middle season (winter), an ending season (spring), followed by a remarkable opportunity for a physical, mental, and emotional wellness reset season (summer). Once that yearly cycle is complete, our school year journey repeats as we start over once again.

Thus, this book is broken down into four parts, or seasons, of a single school year.

- Part 1, Fall: A Season to Renew—Growing Strong in a Season of New Beginnings
- Part 2, Winter: A Season to Be Resolute—Growing Strong in a Season of Heavy Lifting
- Part 3, Spring: A Season to Show Resolve—Growing Strong in a Season of Finishing Well
- Part 4, Summer: A Season to Rejuvenate—Growing Strong in a Season of Rest

Each part or season, in turn, has unique chapters to be used one per week or a whole bunch at a time—whatever works best for your available time and interest. The chapters for each part (season) are numbered 1–13, except for summer. Think of this book as a TV series! Three seasons, each with thirteen episodes, and one season (summer) with eleven. Feel free to jump into the part of the book that corresponds to your current season of the school year (fall, winter, spring, or summer). You can binge-read them if you want, but the pages won't turn until you are ready for the next part of your joy journey!

You will also notice some chapter title oddities. First, each chapter title is one word, unless the title happens to include the word *joy*. Second, some of the titles use unusual words like *gezellig*, *zotheka*, *commuovere*, *meraki*, *naz*, *ubuntu*, *boketto*, and *resfeber*. These words do not have translations directly into English, yet they have a wonderful and culturally expanding impact for understanding joy.

Two *seasonal* caveats to remember as you read. First, your experiences with seasonal weather conditions described in this book may vary by geographical region, proximity to the sun, and the Earth's tilt. Second, your experiences with the *school seasons* of fall, winter, spring, and summer may vary slightly based on when your specific school year (referred to as your school year life) begins and ends. However, no matter where you live and work, or when your school year starts and ends, you can dive into the book during any season to write your own joy story.

Joy is an *acknowledgment* that who you are and what you do matters. Curating your joy involves cultivating a mindset that appreciates and finds worth in the small and ordinary aspects of life. Joy, then, can become an intentional pursuit for your life.

JOY! is intentionally more informal and written in brief snippets, as if we are having a conversation together. Research references and citations are provided at the end of the book as endnotes, so as not to disrupt the flow of your thoughts and reflections.

When I reference *you* in this book, I am including all adults responsible for educating students in your school or district. I am referencing each of us who has chosen the education profession, regardless of our role within the school organization.

I use the phrase *students and colleagues* often. This is intentional. All voices—from school counselor to paraprofessional, from principal to bus driver, from social worker to nurse, from classroom teacher to tech specialist—*matter*. We are all teachers and leaders of one another. Thus, when I use the phrases *students and colleagues* or *teacher and leader*, I mean you. Welcome!

Joy weaves its way through the tapestry of your entire life. All of it. Many reviewers for this book mentioned how impossible it is to separate their personal life from their professional life. How true. My intent is to help you create your own joy manuscript as you build the pathway of your unique life.

Thus, you can use the *MY Joy* spaces in each chapter to write your personal joy narrative or use your favorite notes app if you prefer. These MY Joy spaces are designed as a place to write your thoughts and responses while examining how to present yourself every day with a spark of joy. Use the space provided as you see fit for your personality and journaling style. Share with others as you deem appropriate.

Use this book with colleagues in your professional life as part of a book study. If you do, you will discover and realize your power to be more aware of the circumstances, events, people, places, and strategies that bring joy to your professional and personal life.

Off and on, like me, you will lose connection with the joyful nature of your seasons each school year. You will sometimes teeter and tumble. We all do. It is part of the human experience. Like you, I have been knocked down more than once; yet I have chosen to pursue my *voice and choice for joy*. Joy is at the center of our decision to get back up.

JOY! paints a vision for life—to create and be a part of a joy journey with others. We were created to pursue and give joy. True joy is limitless and life defining—a transformative reservoir waiting to be tapped into season after season.

Join me, will you? Joy connects more than just meaning to life. Joy brings your life, well, to life! Let's crawl, walk, stumble, sprint, rise, and grow strong in a joy journey together. Season after season!

With gratitude,

Tim Kanold

You can check out my video here. I provide personal insights into why I wrote the book, why I chose the format for the book, and why I chose the outline and chapter structure for the book. Thanks for joining the joy journey with me!

PART 1

FALL: A SEASON TO RENEW

Growing Strong in a Season of New Beginnings

Ahh, welcome! It's the beginning of a new school year. Fall represents a time to settle into the rhythm, newness, challenges, and benefits of starting again. As you begin, remember to keep joy at the forefront of your daily life.

You start the new school year with intention toward joy.

You settle into sustainable joy actions as the fall season progresses.

You make the time for joy moments into and through Thanksgiving.

During late August and early September, your work- and home-life activities will ramp up. New beginnings and excitement! Perhaps some anxiety too. There will be new and renewed drains on your fixed amounts of time (it seems there is never enough of it), energy, and attention.

Stress levels will begin to rise. Understanding and using preemptive and self-regulatory joy routines can help with the expectations of higher-level energy needs, unexpected adversity, and the relentless nature of deadlines.

You intuitively know your joy will result from your authentic connection with students, by unleashing their inner genius through creativity, problem solving, and play.[7] Thus, you lean into revised lesson plans from previous school seasons and set up your classroom to create an inviting learning environment. You know, too, that engaging and meaningful lessons are not easy to create and deliver, yet you are determined.

Fall has a certain magic to it—an optimism. You and your colleagues are one year stronger and wiser as you reflect on the lessons learned from previous fall seasons, adjust to new policies and procedures, and yearn for work that really matters. Relationships and bonds are quickly rebuilt as friendships with colleagues are renewed. You collaborate and settle in with joyful relationship routines for the learning and work ahead.

The new school year and fall season present a time of fresh starts, new beginnings. Perhaps this is your very first year as an educator or your first year in a new role, a new school, or a new building. You are reminded of the simple joys of our profession. You observe how your beginning occurs as nature begins to signal its ending. The workplace paradox is not lost on you.

You intuitively know that joy, if not intentionally pursued, can quickly fade away during the fall season. Thus, chapters 1–3 establish the idea of living the busier than normal life ahead through acknowledging the simple joys. Chapters 4–6 remind you of intentional physical- and mental-wellness routines that help sustain joy as the school year progresses. Chapters 7–9 connect you to the journey ahead as you become inspired by and inspiring toward others. Finally, chapters 10–12 provide joy strategies necessary to prepare for the end of the fall season and persevere for the winter season ahead.

Ready? Let's begin!

FALL

Beginnings

Every new beginning comes from some other beginning's end.
—Semisonic

"Welcome back" rings the bell, guiding us to reflect on the new beginnings ahead. If there ever is a time for feeling joy, hope, and excitement in our profession, it should at least occur on opening day, a day of new beginnings, right?

Opening day usually presents optimum moments. It is our chance to start anew and *once again* cultivate meaning and joy with our friends, colleagues, and students. Hope is in the air! "This year will be our best year ever," we think to ourselves and maybe speak it too.

MY JOY

Our previous school year ended just a few short months ago. Here we go again! We dig into our files (digital or otherwise) from a year ago. How did we start last year? What did we learn, what parts of our opening units are staying the same, what strategies are changing, and what did we learn from how well we opened our schools and classrooms this time a year ago?

Describe your best opening-day experience. What happened that made it memorable?

_____
_____
_____
_____
_____
_____
_____
_____
_____
_____
_____
_____

There is a certain energy and buzz in the room as you gather, greet old and new colleagues, renew friendships, and discover life-defining changes: marriages, divorces, babies born, residential moves, new hobbies, career-path changes, birthdays, surgeries, losses, and more. Some we know about—others are surprises. The social gathering feels joyful, yet a little bit edgy. It's like we are at the starting line of a marathon. The long race awaits. Are we ready for it? Maybe, *maybe not*.

"Welcome back!" said the principal up on the stage.

Welcome back from what, exactly? I was not feeling very welcome. I walked into the auditorium and sat down hearing those words, struggling with recent events. I had participated in a nine-day teachers' strike. A rough beginning to a new school year. No one in that room was feeling or choosing joy. The parents in the community had been railing on the teachers, calling us selfish and saying we were unconcerned about their children. I was new to the school district, had just recently accepted the job, and did not yet connect to the past issues between the school and the community. I felt adrift.

The invited speaker was delivering an opening-day message, but I was not paying attention. I was deep in my own thoughts about the seemingly bad decision I had made by accepting the job teaching at this school.

The summer prior to that union strike, I had completed my master's degree in applied mathematics after six years of teaching in a different school district and one year teaching at the university. I wanted to be better prepared to teach high school mathematics.

I had been offered more financially lucrative non-teaching jobs because of that degree. Double the salary and benefits of the new teaching position I had just accepted. That nine-day strike not only cost me nine days of salary, but, as I would learn later, it also kept my salary frozen for the next three years.

In that room, as the guest speaker valiantly tried to maintain our attention, I thought, "What on earth have I done?" We had moved to a new town and uprooted ourselves from our community of friends left behind. My heart could *feel* my joy-based decision to remain in teaching, but my head told me otherwise.

Sounds strange, right?

Despite the strike, despite the severe loss in pay and benefits, in my heart I knew I was wired up to be a teacher. To choose otherwise would have denied my fundamental purpose as a professional.

Research supports that what we *think* will bring us joy—money, status, and achievement—is temporal at best. These things are nice, but their joy impact eventually fades away, leaving us unsatisfied.[8]

Turns out, the most essential elements of our physical wellness (sleep, food, hydration, and movement) and our mental and social wellness (community, gratitude, mindfulness, and meaning) are the elements that bring us *sustained* joy.[9] Teaching was the professional place and space that served my meaning, despite my opening-day experience. Teaching was my place for community—with students, parents, and colleagues.

Joy, by its very nature, is personal. What brings you joy may be different from what brings me joy. However, there are some common ingredients to joy moments along the way. Those ingredients include confidence and credibility (see Spring, Chapter 3: Credibility, page 131) and connection in community with others (see Fall, Chapter 7: Yearning, page 31).[10]

This takes me back to my story.

Despite the hardship felt during my opening-day experience in my new job, I was about to begin the next stage of my journey as a mathematics teacher. I was confident I could inspire high school students.

Although my head was heavy on that opening day, my heart knew I was in the right place. And the next six years of my teaching life at West Chicago were filled with some of the best subsequent seasons of beginnings and endings based on our progress with improved student learning and through the deep and meaningful relationships I experienced with students, colleagues, and staff.

But now, I was moving on to a new beginning in a new school district in Lincolnshire, Illinois. A place that would eventually become known as the birthplace of the Professional Learning Community at Work® (PLC at Work) process we know today.

My family would need to move once again.

I turned in my keys and walked out of that school one last time as emotions washed over me. It was July 27. When my time at that strike-torn school district came to an end, I had invested myself in that community, and I would miss all the persons that brought so much joy to my life. I hugged the incredible office staff—many of them parents in the community—as we said teary goodbyes. They had been part of my professional family. For me, the joy was surely in the work and the people I was privileged to "carry the water with" every day.

I am sure the double-my-salary think-tank job I had been offered six years prior might have contributed to a bigger house, but it would not have met the emotional and joy-filled standards I had set for my life.

MY JOY

Think about your prior opening days.

What part of the new school year strike story resonates most with you?

_____

_____

_____

What are some challenges or adversities you expect to encounter as this new school year begins?

_____

_____

_____

What, for you, are the most joy-filled and exciting aspects of starting the marathon of a new school season despite the potential adversity that looms ahead?

_____

_____

_____

Beginning the new school year is a time for remembering your notes, reflections, and advice from the previous school season. It is also a time of re-membering, or becoming a member again, with your community of colleagues and new students that join you for the long journey of a new school season. That joy connection is next!

FALL

Remember

Life is about reconnecting with others and with the world around you. Embrace the opportunity to become a member again, and let your journey unfold with connection and renewed purpose.

—Anonymous

Re-member. To become a member once again.

I loved playing softball in the fall league once the new school year began. Double-header games on Tuesday nights in September. Sometimes, we would be assigned the late games at 8:30 p.m. and 9:30 p.m. The lights would be on, and the fog would hang close as the warm ground met with the cooler air.

More importantly, none of the guys I played softball with cared less about what I did for a living. We came from all neighborhoods, backgrounds, and walks of life; our common membership existing around a twelve-inch, round ball—hitting, catching, and throwing it.

The stress of my day would dissipate under the weight of our laughter, our competitiveness, our limitations, and our ability to make fun of and accept one another. We were in our forties by then, older guys who had once been pretty good athletes; we now just wanted to hang on and create a few more good memories before it was too late. We would remember and re-member (become members once again) every fall at a local softball diamond in that Park District fall league.

Write about your favorite weekly activity for spending time with friends outside your workplace.

_____
_____
_____
_____
_____
_____
_____
_____
_____
_____
_____
_____
_____
_____
_____
_____
_____
_____
_____
_____
_____
_____
_____
_____
_____
_____

I still have my long-sleeved T-shirt from the year we surprised ourselves and won that fall league. And I have a team picture from the local newspaper framed on my office wall. For nineteen years, those friends outside my work life provided just the place I needed to let go of my more unpleasant emotions of fear and anxiety, sadness and pain, and stress and strain from life's pressures.

Occasionally, I will wear that worn-out T-shirt, read the names under our team picture, and allow myself to remember how much I valued the balm those men and the weekly routines offered me—without judgment, without shame, without comparison—as we morphed into a collection of like-minded, kind, and reasonably successful souls.

MY J O Y

My story is about becoming a member of a team outside of work, and re-membering with them every fall. This is similar to your experiences at the beginning of a new school year as you become a member of your school, your classroom, and your collaborative team once again.

Fall, then, is a time to re-member with others and make agreements together to *not* let the everyday stress, fear, pain, sadness, frustration, shame, embarrassment, or comparison win the day. These not-so-pleasant states of being can eat away at an effective start to your new school year.

Fall is a time to remember weekly joy-building routines that are so good for bringing your best self to work each day, as the renewed pace of life settles in. Ready for a weekly list of well-being routines to sustain?

MY JOY

Answer the following questions; then write about your results.

1. How many *physical well-being* routines can you check off at least five to six times per week?
    a. Getting seven hours or more of sleep per night
    b. Moving, exercising, or playing sports
    c. Drinking at least six cups of water per day

2. How many *mental or emotional well-being* routines can you check off at least three to four times per week?
    a. Pursuing hobbies in art, music, cooking, gaming, reading, and so on
    b. Engaging in mindfulness routines, such as journaling or breathing
    c. Sitting in silence and solitude for fifteen minutes or more

3. How many *social well-being* routines can you check off at least one to two times per week?
    a. Spending time with family members outside of your household
    b. Spending time with friends outside of your workplace
    c. Getting outside and spending time in nature

My results for each of the nine routines listed:

_____
_____
_____
_____
_____
_____
_____
_____
_____
_____
_____
_____
_____
_____

How many of the nine weekly, joy-building actions were you able to check off? I hit six of nine while writing this chapter. These nine routines represent intentional wellness actions that support simple joys during the hustle and bustle of your daily life. Write about some next steps you can take for the routines you identified in need of improvement.

Pursuing these weekly routines provides pockets of joy waiting to be rediscovered. Each intentional moment of seeking and savoring your connections with others around well-being routines becomes a road map toward infusing your days with a touch of joy.

Understanding your life within the context of *simple joy* is next.

FALL

Simple Joy

Enjoy the little things, for one day you may look back and realize they were the big things.

—Robert Brault

As you move into this new school year, remember your joy does not need to be complicated. Yet, it does need to be intentional. Some days are so exasperating and complicated that joy is left in the dust of your path.

We were two weeks into the new school year, and I had a lot on my mind as I started my twenty-six-mile drive to work in silence, fuming a little because of an argument that morning with my—at the time—eighth-grade son. The tension was hanging in the air with no resolution in sight when I had to head off to work.

I was also low on gas, so I pulled into my normal gas station, filled up the tank, got a cup of coffee, and took off again. I was now running late. As I took off, I could hear this thumping sound against the side of my car. I ignored it. It got louder. I glanced at my driver's side mirror, and to my horror, the gas pump hose was still attached to my gas tank opening, and the end of the hose was hitting the side of my car. In that moment, I imagined gas pouring out of the gas station pump a half mile back.

I headed back to the gas station, sheepishly turned in their hose, and was given some grace when the attendant said to me, "That's OK, honey. It happens about twice a week." Misery loves company. I did not know there was an automatic shutoff valve for just such an event, so everything and everyone was safe!

What do you imagine when you hear the phrase *simple joy*?

_____
_____
_____
_____
_____
_____
_____
_____
_____
_____
_____
_____
_____
_____
_____
_____
_____
_____
_____
_____
_____
_____
_____
_____
_____

Now, I was super late and walked into our morning guiding coalition meeting after it had already started. The meeting discussions left me with an exhaustive to-do list as I headed out to teach my third-period calculus class. I knew my students would be anxiously awaiting the results of their unit tests from the day before, which I did not grade, partially because the argument with my son the previous evening had bled over into the morning.

It was 11:30 a.m. with a long day still ahead.

At this point, I made a lunchtime decision. Go outside. Sit by yourself and journal. Take a deep breath and step back for twenty minutes. The afternoon needs you to be better, to be intentional, to cut through the noise, and to get small. To find a few *simple* joys.

What are simple joys?

MY JOY

Our *joy journey* is defined as a state of mind to be cultivated independent of your circumstances, including times of grief, stress, or uncertainty (see the introduction, page 1). Sometimes our joy journey can feel complicated, elusive.

Simple joy, however, cuts like a knife through the phrase, *It's complicated*. *Simple* as an adjective indicates an idea that is easy to understand, uncomplicated, or not complex.[11] It refers to something straightforward, basic, and lacking unnecessary intricacies or complications. Simple joy, then, involves cultivating a mindset that appreciates and finds joy in the small and ordinary aspects of life—each day, despite the noise, stress, and complications of your daily grind.

Simple joy is a straightforward *acknowledgment* that who you are and what you do *matters*, especially on the days when a gasoline pump hose is hitting the side of your car, you are arguing with your son, and you cannot catch up to the pace of your day.

There is a body of neuroscience and psychology research that supports the idea of finding simple joy in your experiences by intentionally engaging in activities that help mitigate the detrimental effects of chronic stress and strain on the brain. The emerging evidence supports the idea that cultivating a positive mindset by engaging in various mindfulness routines can contribute to your daily mental well-being and neurological health.[12]

Simple joy, then, is derived from finding delight in small, everyday moments and acknowledging life's adventures. Simple joy occurs when you spend time with loved ones, enjoy nature, savor a good meal, or engage in activities that bring a sense of contentment and fulfillment. The essence of simple joy lies in appreciating the little things that contribute to a positive and enjoyable life.

I sat down at that lunchtime picnic table and journaled about how much I loved teaching my students. Yes, they cut me some slack after I asked if they remembered what it was like to be in junior high and how they felt about *their* parents during those early teen years. They gave me plenty of parenting advice. I wrote about their funny responses.

I noticed the quiet around me except for the sound of a lawnmower off in the distance and the smell of the newly cut late-summer, early-fall grass around my feet. I *love* that smell!

I wrote about how much I deeply loved my son too. Then I stood up, determined to be a better father that evening and listen to my son's perspective. His final statement to me that morning, "Dad, you listen to me, but you don't hear me," had merit. Simple joy was in acknowledging these small benefits of life all around me despite the craziness of the day behind me and in front of me. Cultivating a positive mindset and telling him how much I loved him was a gift I promised to give myself and him in the moment of *that* day.

MY JOY ♥

Describe a moment in your life when a daily routine of stepping away briefly allowed you to appreciate the simple things that contribute to a positive and enjoyable life.

___
___
___
___
___
___
___
___

Write about how you cultivate a positive mindset at work and how you pay attention to your surroundings, engaging your senses.

Speaking of simple joy: Those twenty minutes at the picnic table gave me some space to breathe and sit in an outdoor environment as I listened to music. Remembering the simple joys of breathing, nature, and music is the focus of the next three chapters. Let's go!

FALL

Breathe

Feelings come and go like clouds in a windy sky.
Conscious breathing is my anchor.
—Thich Nhat Hanh

As this fall season moves you forward, take a moment to step back and remember with your daily breathing. Yes, your breathing! It will bring you back to a place of calm and well-being. Those high-stress days that are sure to occur do not need to rob you of your joy in *that* day.

"Don't forget to breathe."

My colleague Tina Boogren said these words to me during a Zoom conversation. As a runner, I was pretty sure I knew how to breathe; it is essential to running well. And yet, I was about to get a lesson on how to breathe as a connector to joy in my day!

We were working on a section of our *Educator Wellness* book, routines for cultivating mindfulness.[13] We were discussing strategies that would help remove—or at least diminish—the intensity of anxiety and stress one might feel from more unpleasant emotions, such as guilt, anger, frustration, or feeling overwhelmed.

One strategy Tina wanted to discuss in the book was mindful breathing. Based on our conversation, the following ideas eventually worked their way into our book. Her wisdom significantly improved my daily breathing routines.

It might help to "take a deep inhale through your nose, pause, then deeply exhale through your mouth, pause, and repeat.... Try to push your breath into your belly so that your stomach expands on the inhale."[14] Mindful breathing calms your nervous system, reduces stress, increases alertness, and boosts your immune system.[15]

Because of my appreciation for Tina's wisdom in our work, I allowed my skepticism to succumb and to keep an open mind about placing an intentional focus on my breathing techniques. I slowly began to practice box breathing as needed, which seemed to be most days.

Box breathing, also known as square breathing or four-square breathing, is a simple and effective exercise that involves equalizing the four phases of breathing—inhaling, holding the breath, exhaling, and holding the breath again. This technique is often used as a mindfulness and relaxation exercise to manage stress, reduce anxiety, and promote a sense of calm.

Here's a step-by-step guide to box breathing.[16]

1. *Inhale (count to four):* Start by taking a slow, deep breath through your nose, counting to four as you inhale. Focus on filling your lungs with air and expanding your diaphragm.
2. *Hold (count to four):* After inhaling, hold your breath for a count of four. Keep your lungs filled and maintain a sense of stillness during this pause.
3. *Exhale (count to four):* Slowly exhale through your mouth or nose for a count of four. Release the air from your lungs in a controlled manner.
4. *Hold (count to four):* After exhaling, hold your breath again for a count of four. Embrace the brief pause before beginning the next inhalation.
5. *Repeat:* Continue this cycle of box breathing for several rounds, gradually increasing the duration of each cycle if comfortable. Focus on the rhythmic pattern and maintain a steady pace.

You can practice box breathing anywhere or anytime, making it a convenient tool for managing moments of tension or anxiety. Regular practice of box breathing may also contribute to your overall well-being and sense of joy.[17]

According to Emma Seppälä at the Yale School of Management, changing your breathing patterns can change your emotions.[18] If, during the day, your anxiety intensifies, you will notice short, irregular, and fast breaths. Adopting a slower, more regular breathing pattern, such as the box-breathing technique, can promote a calm feeling.

MY JOY

The slower, regular breathing pattern, especially the longer exhale, "activat[es] the vagus nerve, slowing heart rate, easing blood pressure, and settling you down."[19] Breathing like this works, Seppälä says, because "it actively relaxes your physiological state."[20]

Remember, your joy journey is defined as *a state of mind to be cultivated independent of your circumstances, including times of grief, stress, or uncertainty* (see the introduction, page 1). Give yourself the daily gift of mindful breathing. It will improve your mood and keep you steady on your joy journey as the fall season unfolds.

I have added box breathing to my daily run, and it was *hard* to do in the beginning. Yet, it has helped me to maintain a steady state, despite the stress being placed on my body, and has improved my overall sense of joy through my observations of gradual physical and mental improvement. This, in turn, gives me the confidence to keep trying.

Try it! Practice box breathing, and then write about your experience.

MY JOY

How can you use intentional breathing to impact your joy journey at work and at home each day?

_____
_____
_____
_____
_____
_____
_____
_____
_____
_____
_____
_____
_____
_____
_____
_____
_____
_____
_____
_____
_____
_____
_____
_____
_____
_____

As you move into and through October, colors might begin to change depending on where you live. No matter what, don't forget to take time to see, smell, and breathe in the joy of nature all around you. Take a moment to go outside and look around. The serenity of nature tends to ground your present concerns and allows you the space and place to connect to and cultivate your joy. The joy-nature connection is next!

FALL

Nature

We are seeing changes in the brain and changes in the body that suggest we are physically and mentally more healthy when we are interacting with nature.

—David Strayer

Sometimes, in the fall season, nature reaches out as we settle into yearlong joy routines.

It was late September, and I woke up, made a cup of coffee, and looked outside my hotel window. It was dark, rainy, and windy. Not an ideal fall morning. I checked the weather app on my phone, and saw it was 42 degrees Fahrenheit with winds close to nineteen miles per hour. Rainy *and* cold. Not the best combination for heading outside.

Yet, head outside I must.

I was on a hot streak of starting my mornings with making time before work to be outside. I craved the daily fifteen to thirty minutes out in the quiet of my surroundings, going for a brief walk and listening to the sounds of the early morning. Being outside in whatever nature had to offer, starting my day by reconnecting to my acknowledgment of my daily life and the often hectic and intense action around and in front of me—the stress and the joy. Only now, my streak was about to be broken. I had not brought clothes for this kind of weather.

It was dark when I arrived at the hotel the night before (I was working with an out-of-state school district the next day), and all I could see of any "nature" around me was a series of

What has been the craziest (and intentional) action you have taken to give yourself the gift of some time with nature and to capture a moment of joy outside during the fall season?

_____
_____
_____
_____
_____
_____
_____
_____
_____
_____
_____
_____
_____
_____
_____
_____
_____
_____
_____
_____
_____
_____

parking lots attached to six national chain hotels. I stood looking out my small window, frustrated. I couldn't see much of nature, I couldn't hear nature's sounds, and more importantly—for me at least—I couldn't smell any of the wonderful aromas of nature from inside my room. Sometimes, on my best morning walks, I swear I can taste the cool and crisp air.

I was bummed.

In desperation—and running out of time to get ready for the teaching day ahead—an idea occurred to me. I dressed in my "inside" workout clothes, kept on my pajama bottoms, and went down to the front desk. I explained the dilemma to the night clerk (it was 4:45 a.m.) and asked her if she had a coat and an umbrella I could borrow. The coat didn't fit, but the umbrella would give me some relief. However, she had a blanket she could give me!

I headed out into the parking lot, searching for a little bit of nature. My appearance was strange, I was sure, but I felt the promise of feeling more alive to start this day.

MY JOY

Do you love spending time outside, especially during the fall? There's something about the simplicity of nature that resonates with us. Would you agree? Whether it's feeling the warmth of the fall sun on your face, listening to the sound of the wind in the trees, or taking in the natural scenery around you, being outside rarely fails to bring a deeper sense of joy. Being outside is a go-to place for renewing your energy, where you can appreciate the beauty often overlooked due to the relentless nature (pun intended) of your daily life.

The research connecting nature and joy implies that nature offers a free resource (like when we walk out the door with a blanket and umbrella) that contributes to our mental well-being. Nature has a profound impact on our brains and our behavior, helping us to *reduce* anxiety, rumination (focused attention on negative aspects of life), and stress. The benefits of spending time in nature include increased attention and awareness capacity, increased creativity, and improvement in our ability to connect with others (like our necessary relationships with students and colleagues).[21]

Fall reveals a paradox, right? In our professional life, the school year is just beginning. Yet, in our personal life, nature is serving up an ending. Leaves are falling; colors are signaling one last burst of energy before the end of this cycle of their life, only for the deciduous trees to go dormant for the winter. Nature, it seems, has its own timing of beginnings and endings, depending on where you live in the world.

Nature also serves as a source of rejuvenation, inspiration, and emotional fulfillment. Through those quiet morning walks outside, we can shift to a more positive and joyful outlook on the day. We are each part of an educator's work life and humanity, trying to walk our daily path.

So, what happened that fall morning when I ventured into the parking lot wilderness? The first thing I noticed as I walked around those hotels was the scent of wet, damp, fallen leaves. It was earthy—musky in a way. It had a distinctive aroma. That scent is always nostalgic for me, taking me back to fall seasons from my past and bringing an awareness that the seasons really are changing.

While wandering, I found a path behind one of the hotels that led me to some woods. The path wasn't very long—maybe four hundred yards—but I was immersed in the woods and up on a hill. I could see the outlines of hundreds of tall trees to my left and the lights of homes waking up down the hill to my right. I walked the path back and forth three times and then headed back through the parking lots to get ready to start my day. The quiet had been reassuring. Peaceful. My depleted attention circuits from the day before restored.

I was ready to go, wet blanket and all.

MY JOY

How can you be more intentional about getting out into nature to recapture, renew, and maintain your joy journey; let go of your stress; and improve your connection with students and colleagues? Who might you invite to walk with you before or after school?

_____
_____
_____
_____
_____
_____
_____
_____
_____
_____
_____
_____
_____
_____
_____
_____
_____
_____
_____
_____
_____
_____
_____
_____
_____

Sometimes, during the quiet of my nature walks, I will play some music. Music can inspire our mood. Making the time for music in your life is perhaps one of the greatest sources of joy, ever. That aspect of your joy journey is next!

FALL

Music

To stop the flow of music would be like the stopping of time itself, incredible and inconceivable.

—Aaron Copland

We are listening, playing, and dancing to a lot of music these days. More than 436,000 tracks were streamed more than one million times on Spotify in 2023—a 33.7 percent increase from 2022. There are a staggering number of songs and artists with incredible worldwide reach thanks to the availability of music streaming and the freedom to upload offered by digital distributors. More than seven trillion songs total streamed in 2023.[22]

MY JOY

Whether it's classical, jazz, soft rock, hard rock, pop, hip hop, rap, heavy metal, R&B, country, folk, punk, and more, we each have our favorite genres, musicians, albums, or playlists. Music has a purpose in our lives. It brings us together and provides joy. We feel it. We move to it. Every brain needs music.

There is a period during adolescence where we form strong ties to different types of music. What we like and dislike can change over the course of our lives,

What is it about listening to or dancing to music that brings you the most joy?

_____
_____
_____
_____
_____

What type of music do you most enjoy? What's residing in your playlist?

_____
_____
_____
_____
_____

but there are certain patterns of music we get attached to when we are young.[23]

Listening to music has been associated with the activation of dopaminergic pathways in the brain. Dopamine, a neurotransmitter linked to pleasure and reward, is released during enjoyable experiences, including the appreciation and pleasure derived from music. Functional magnetic resonance imaging (fMRI) studies show that various brain regions involved in emotional processing light up. The amygdala, hippocampus, and prefrontal cortex contribute to our emotional and cognitive joy experienced through music.[24]

Think about the last concert you attended with friends or family members. When you listen to music with others, your brain exhibits neural synchronization. This phenomenon involves the alignment of brainwave patterns among individuals, fostering a sense of connection and shared emotional experiences, enhancing the joy derived by your communal listening and participation in the music.[25] Music enhances your life experiences at work and at home and has the capacity to bring us together to communicate our stories for generations to come.

This notion of shared experiences is why Gabriel Fauré's Requiem comes to mind. Or, more specifically, "Requiem in D minor, Op. 48."[26] It is my best memory of my father during and shortly after my high school years. We had had some good but mostly difficult days during my senior year, as we rarely talked to one other.

He was a classically trained musician who was often on the road. His schedule and interests were different from mine. I was more into sports and sang as a side hobby. He was more into music and didn't engage in sports. Yet we shared one activity in common.

To make extra money, my dad worked in various churches that needed a temporary choral director. He would work six to eight months until the church found a permanent director, and then he would move on to another church. No matter the church, faith, or denomination, I always showed up, sometimes singing in five services on a Sunday morning. I showed up because it was the one place I knew I could be with him, and we most likely would not argue.

Once I headed off to college, I would still head out to whatever church he was working at, for special occasions. For my dad, music was his place of joy. When I was nineteen, despite my vocal limitations, he asked me to join him for a church performance of Fauré's Requiem. It was in Latin and a challenging piece of music. It is about death—a slow and sad piece, yet deeply moving.

When I close my eyes, I can still hear the two of us singing together that evening. It was the only time we sang together before he passed away. Sometimes, I sing the opening to the Requiem, and through the sound of my voice, I hear my father singing. Although the music is sad, it always brings me joy.

I have learned, of course, to move my musical tastes outside of classical. I love the music of Jimmy Buffett, Aretha Franklin, Amy Grant, the Eagles, The Temptations, Sting, Billy Joel, Chance the Rapper, Lady Gaga, John Legend, Elton John, and many more. Yet I am aware my musical sense is limited, as most of my family members are not very interested in my playlists.

My son, however, is a master at building playlists we all seem to like. I finally asked him to share a playlist I could use when I am on the road speaking at events. Shortly after I placed his songs into the opening and closing of my sessions, audience members started complimenting me on how my playlists rock! I am quick to give him the credit.

So, here you are. You are about two months into the new school season. Somehow, the fall season doesn't feel quite so *new* anymore. School life is settling in. You are most likely experiencing some long days.

You head home. Car, train, bus, bicycle, walking . . . it doesn't matter. You intentionally decide to lighten and brighten your mood. You choose joy. You crank up your favorite playlist and listen to some music. You scroll through your artists and albums, Apple Music, Spotify, FM, or XM radio, and hit *play*. Before you know it, you are moving to the music. Maybe you are laughing and belting out the tune or crying as you connect to a past memory. You are experiencing the motion and the emotion—the joy—of that music.

The stress and the strain of this late fall day does not get the best of you. The music and the movement—the dopamine and serotonin release, the subsequent joy—win!

MY JOY

Today, think about the music you love. What are some life hacks that bring the joy of music to your home, your classroom, your school, your celebrations, your friends, and your family? Make music *together* today! And share!

Sometimes as I listen to music, a subtle yearning will arise. It seems strange to me, as I am not always sure—is it about a connection to something greater than me, is it about something from my past, or is it about something in my future that I long for?

Yearning has a positive connection to joy. And that discussion is next!

FALL

Yearning

Joy itself, considered simply as an event in my own mind, turned out to be of no value at all. All the value lay in that of which Joy was the desiring.

—C. S. Lewis

"Why do we have to set goals and create an action plan together?"

This is a question I have been asked hundreds of times (usually during the fall season) by preK–12 teacher teams in all settings: rural, urban, and suburban; elementary, middle, and high school.

And not until now has my answer been *joy*. Or, more specifically, *yearning*.

Yes, yearning.

Joy is often understood through the lens of an event. The joy of that concert, a classroom celebration with students, a gift of clothes or jewelry, or maybe a weekend getaway. Yet joy is often found in your experiences from the preparation, toil, and effort leading up to that event. Yearning conveys a depth of joy beyond a simple wish or hope. Yearning is "a tender or urgent longing" and is connected to joy in a more complex and nuanced way.[27]

While yearning itself may imply a sense of longing or desire for something yet to be attained (student learning goals, for example), the *fulfillment* of that yearning (and the journey to get there) has the potential to bring profound joy.

That student learning goal plan you submit creates anticipation for the journey ahead. Can your team work *together* over the next few weeks or months of the school year to achieve the desired student learning outcomes you have set? Moreover, when you realize success toward your yearning (or longing) for that new level of student performance,

What do you currently yearn for at work in terms of improved student learning outcomes appropriate to your job responsibilities?

_____
_____
_____
_____
_____
_____
_____
_____
_____
_____
_____
_____
_____
_____
_____
_____
_____
_____
_____
_____
_____
_____
_____

you most likely will celebrate the results. That celebration also provides a source of joy.

MY JOY

Thus, the connection between yearning and joy is found in anticipating reaching the goal as part of the journey. Yearning is rooted in our desire to find meaning in our work through our students' eventual achievements. There becomes an emotional connection to our short- and long-term wins through the school year.

There is research that explores the neural mechanisms associated with desire and motivation, which are related to the experience of yearning. One relevant area of research involves the brain's reward system, particularly the mesolimbic dopamine pathway.[28]

Dopamine, a neurotransmitter, plays a crucial role in our brain's reward and pleasure circuits. When we anticipate or experience rewards, such as the fulfillment of our short- or long-term goals, the release of dopamine contributes to positive reinforcement and joy.[29]

Interestingly, the *actions* we take on our goals and plans serve our joy-yearning connection by creating conditions that can lead to joy at work.

- *Anticipation:* The joy in yearning is found in the anticipation that we might meet our chosen goal. The prospect of attaining what we long for (more students performing at grade level, for example) can evoke a sense of excitement and positive expectation, contributing to the joy associated with the process. The joy is literally in the journey itself.
- *Achievement:* When the yearning is fulfilled, and our desired goal or experience is attained, this can bring a deep and fulfilling joy. Party time! The contrast between the initial yearning (goal plan and action) and the realization of the desired student learning outcomes (achievement of the goal) enhances the positive emotional reward.

- *Meaning and purpose:* Yearning for something meaningful, such as connection to the reason we are showing up for work each day (improved student learning), can lead to a profound and lasting joy when our deeper aspiration of student learning is fulfilled.

So, why do we yearn?

Neuroscience suggests our brains are wired to crave what we don't have. Dopamine is released when we get what we want, but even more is released when we anticipate getting what we want.[30] Setting goals sparks our anticipation! To experience joy, anticipation does not require a guaranteed payoff. When we work with our team toward a common student learning goal, not knowing if we will reach the goal does not take away from the joy of the effort and our potential to reach that goal.

There is one caveat, however.

Once we get what we want (we reach the student achievement goal), the dopamine fades—and so we yearn for more. Thus, we *set a new goal for the next season ahead* to keep the joy-yearning connection alive.

Essentially, the PLC mantra of *forever improvement* produces a continual dopamine release as you anticipate and then achieve the journey toward those improved student learning outcomes in your goals and plans.

MY JOY

When working with your team, what brings you the most joy? The *anticipation*, the *achievement*, or the connection to your greater *purpose*?

Student learning goals aside, write about what you yearn for as part of your personal or professional journey. Perhaps it is a specific job, location, team achievement, use of the latest technology, or creating a more inclusive classroom. Set a goal, create a plan, and then enjoy the anticipation and the achievement that lies ahead!

This chapter used the pronouns *we* and *our*. These words send a message of *us*—*our* team, *our* togetherness, *our* learning, and *our* relationship toward a common goal. Creating joyful shared experiences and emotional connections that enrich our daily work life can be challenging but well worth the effort as we march through October. That joy connection is next!

FALL

Relationships

A great relationship is about two things: first, appreciating the similarities, and second, respecting the differences.
—Maya Angelou

Sometimes, it is hard to let go.

I stood in his office as he was saying goodbye. We had worked together for twenty-two years, and he was about to walk out the door. We hugged, which was unusual because he wasn't the hugging type. He had started out as my mentor, and we quickly realized a deep connection around shared experiences designed to help every student learn. And we were different, for sure. I was mathematics, and he was social studies. He was brilliant—me not so much. I was highly relational, and he was working on it.

As we shook hands and he got ready to go, I realized that somewhere in our journey together, we began to provide one another emotional support—support without judgment, especially during difficult and adverse times.

The line between mentor and mentee eventually became blurred. I remember crossing the line to share a more equal power in our relationship late at night in a coffee shop. We had a quiet shared moment revealing our vulnerabilities, wanting to be better. Building trust. Feeling emotionally and physically secure in our relationship. No matter what we were going through, we could rely on each other for a more positive and joyful outlook on life.

My eyes were a bit misty as he got into his car, waved goodbye one last time, and drove off our campus. His office was now my office. I was taking over for a living legend and not quite sure if I could do the job. And yet he had encouraged my personal growth and development (as well as that of a thousand others). We had achieved a lot *together*, but more importantly, we had learned a lot *together*, school season after school season.

I sat down in his chair (now my chair) and thought about how our friendship soared despite not having many common interests or activities outside of our profession. We engaged in and enjoyed different sports, different hobbies, different music, and different circles of friends, yet the sharing of those variant experiences deepened our bond. We had become confidants—the highest level of friendship.

Just the week before, as he was packing up and getting ready to go, I asked him what he would miss most about our school and district after twenty years of leading the way.

His answer was swift.

The people. The relationships. The community. The collaborative pursuit of excellence. The emotional energy of our school life.

He had given us a master class in how to create social networks, engage with the entire school community, and allow *individuals to connect* with others as we built an incredible professional learning community of adults for the express purpose of improved student learning. Long before neuroscience confirmed it, he understood the power of social interactions and community as a link to increased happiness, well-being, and joy at work.[31]

On my drive home, I could not get the image of that final goodbye out of my head. It seemed odd that it took the finality of his leaving to help me realize how much I loved him. Love is a powerful force that brings joy to our relationships. Whether it's romantic love, familial love, or friendship love like I had with him, the experience of feeling loved and loving others is the fundamental source of joy we experience through our relationships.

The day my friend and mentor walked out the door was a long time ago, yet it seems like yesterday. My positive emotional response in that moment was *not* about the unprecedented level of student learning achieved or the incredible recognition and multiple awards our faculty and staff received as individuals and as a collective. Yes, we celebrated the achievements of our journey every step of the way. But our laser focus was the deep sense of community and relationship that got us there.

That was the source of joy I felt as he left our campus for the final time.

Right about now, as you are moving through October, adapting to adverse circumstances can start to wear you down, right? By this point in the fall season, relationships can become strained. They require work and may need more of your attention. You wonder, *Is the effort worth it?*

MY JOY

And yet, the worst joy decision you can make is to go at it alone. Or, to lean away from your more difficult relationships at work. Loneliness is the opposite of strong relationships and is harmful to your physical and mental health.[32] Strong relationships are part of a joy decision that makes you healthier. Equally as important, striving for self-achievement is fine, but the joy from self-achievement is temporary. Striving for experiences and achievements *with others* is the long-term joy goal.[33]

Hmm. Experiences and relationships triumph over self-achievement and isolation?

Absolutely. Very little that is positive in life is solitary. Relationships with *other people* are the best antidote to the downs of life and are the single most-reliable up.[34]

You have chosen a profession that is about experiences of learning (yours, your students, and your colleagues) through effective relationships and connections with others. When you operate every day within an authentic and positive professional learning *community*, you end up participating in one of the most powerful and joyful professions.

This was the gift given to others by my colleague and friend when he walked out that door and brought the PLC at Work movement to the world.[35] In that moment, I understood there were several *actions* I could take to maintain healthy relationships and continue their potential to bring joy to my journey.

Describe a time when you had a final goodbye with a colleague or team member.

_____
_____
_____
_____
_____
_____
_____
_____
_____
_____
_____
_____
_____
_____
_____
_____
_____
_____
_____
_____
_____
_____
_____
_____
_____
_____

Joy connections are based on the following.

- Sharing experiences about life
- Sharing moments of joy through frequent celebrations
- Knowing that celebrating *experiences* lasts longer than the joy of celebrating achievements
- Giving and receiving emotional support during good and challenging times
- Knowing the security of someone you can trust at work
- Cheering personal growth and development—a hallmark of successful teams
- Connecting with others to build community
- Embracing love as the fundamental source of joy in relationships

MY JOY

Read the joy connections list before this MY Joy prompt. Which relationship actions most resonate with and matter to you? Why?

_____
_____
_____
_____
_____
_____
_____
_____
_____

Describe your current *intentional* actions for improving your relationships at work.

_____
_____
_____
_____
_____
_____
_____
_____

When Rick DuFour said goodbye to me and walked out that door for the final time, he understood the need for habituation. And that joy connection is next!

FALL

Habituation

Habituation. It may be as fundamental a characteristic of life as DNA.

—Vincent Dethier

It's November! If we are not careful, joy can lose its illumination. Sustaining joy can be tough! Complete the next MY Joy prompt, and trust me, it has a point!

MY JOY

It was my ninth fall season of teaching when I noticed, sometime around early November (right after Halloween), my students became less and less enthusiastic about my lesson design and classroom process. I also noticed my own tendency to become a bit numb to the routine of my daily work life.

Another set of lessons and assessments. Another day. Day after day.

Don't get me wrong, I love teaching, and I love mathematics. My work serves my joy, but I would settle into the school year, and it would start to feel mundane. The exhilaration at the start of the new school year had dissipated.

Write about a time when you went on vacation and how great it felt when you returned home.

_____
_____
_____
_____
_____
_____
_____
_____
_____
_____
_____
_____
_____
_____

The daily drumbeat of my work life, the drone of my schedule, and the never-changing rhythm of each day seemed to have a negative impact on my joy journey with students. Conversations with my colleagues at a series of endless and repeated meetings with the same rituals and processes were necessary but a bit mind-numbing.

At the time, I did not know much about how my brain responded to various stimuli. I had not heard of the word *habituation*, yet that is exactly what was happening to me. I loved teaching and wanted my job. But now that I had my job and the year had started, the excitement had worn off, and it didn't seem to satisfy me quite as much.

So, what did I do about it? How could I bring a sense of joy back to my students and the classroom? In a way, could I bring back that feeling of newness and excitement from just a few months ago?

I turned to my coaching background for insight. I was the sophomore boys' basketball coach at the high school. Practices usually lasted two hours. Like the classroom, each practice had a rhythm to it for warm-up drills performing essential skills, breakouts by position groups, and then half-court and full-court scrimmages. I tried hard to model elements of effective teaching—well-organized, efficient, with constant movement and involvement by the players and coaches. No standing around, no wasted time.

Like my classroom teaching, eventually the daily practices lost their novelty and impact. Drills became routine, and players responded to the routines by going through the motions. Not a lot of intensity. It drove me crazy.

Yet, I was keenly aware that the lack of intensity was my issue to resolve. Thus, I routinely changed warm-up drills and made the guards play the forward positions and vice versa. I brought in a different team for our scrimmages or added timing and music to our drills. Sometimes, I made them play an entire scrimmage without being allowed to dribble the basketball. Or I created rotations from station to station through various timed drills. I wanted every practice to have something new—an odd twist to the mundane.

And then, when we went back to our usual routine, the players were so glad things were back to "normal" for a while!

This is the secret to fighting off habituation. When we habituate, "we respond less and less to stimuli that repeat."[36] For example, imagine finding immense joy at the start of that vacation you wrote about in the MY Joy section at the beginning of this chapter.

After a few days on vacation, the initial excitement or pleasure associated with the sights, sounds, and locations of that vacation will decrease as habituation sets in. This doesn't necessarily mean that your joy disappears entirely, but the emotional response tends to be less intense as the vacation progresses.

Remember when you left home to start that vacation? Home had become somewhat mundane. The same setting and routines for daily meals, sleeping, working, laundry, cleaning, and so on. You couldn't wait to leave home and go on that vacation! Your brain was screaming for new stimuli!

And now, when you come home from that vacation, it suddenly feels so good to be home! Home is now providing a renewed set of stimuli (and perhaps an appreciation of the comforts of home as well). The connection between habituation and joy lies in the potential for habituation, no matter how good our circumstances are, to influence our positive emotional responses over time.

Our joy in the classroom may diminish without designing lessons that provide variety, novelty, and mindful appreciation of diverse student learning experiences. The vacation scenario is one of four *temporary actions* you can take to prevent habituation from settling into your classroom routines.

1. *Temporarily change the environment or atmosphere:* Change the desk arrangement in your classroom, take students outside on a nice fall day, use technology or don't use technology, use music and soundscapes or lighting changes during the lesson, engage in interactive work (via labs and so on), or use student-created displays.
2. *Temporarily change the rules:* Use learning stations so students can rotate from station to station to learn skills for the lesson or unit. You can also use a role reversal with a student-led or taught set of lessons or game day rules to enhance the learning of review standards.
3. *Temporarily change classroom interaction routines:* Switch classrooms occasionally with a colleague and teach their classes for the day, while they teach yours. Allow students to move around and engage with new partners for the day.
4. *Temporarily take real or imaginary mini-breaks:* Give students a two-minute brain break to stand up and move around or a five-minute break to discuss their favorite non-content-related topic.

The interplay between habituation and joy will grow stronger as you intentionally (and temporarily) change your routines. Emphasis should be on variety, novelty, and mindful appreciation of diverse experiences to sustain your joy journey over time. By consciously introducing new elements into your daily routine (for example, taking a different route to work), you can mitigate the impact of habituation on your subjective well-being.

MY JOY

Which of the four *temporary changes* represents your greatest "fighting off habituation" strength at work or at home? Which one represents an area for improvement? Write or share with someone about it.

_____
_____
_____
_____
_____
_____
_____
_____
_____
_____
_____
_____
_____
_____
_____
_____
_____
_____
_____
_____

Thank goodness for the break from habituation of our overall work lives during the summer season. It allows us to come back each school year renewed and refreshed. However, it is more difficult to find the time during the school year to temporarily change our routines. "I can't find the time" becomes a familiar refrain as the fall clock ticks forward. Joy, however, finds its strength when we decide how to *make* the time. That's next!

FALL

Time

*In this short Life that only lasts an hour
How much—how little—is within our power*
                            —Emily Dickinson

You are getting deeper into the fall season. It is in full swing now. You can feel the weight of not having enough time to get everything done. Time is your biggest currency, and you do not have enough of it. It marches on, dragging you along into what seems like a relentless string of days and nights with not enough sleep during the school season.

The funny thing about time is, as the adage goes, it waits for no one. And it is fixed. There are 1,440 minutes each day. No more, no less. Unlike our energy, which is renewable, time can be a resource that feels scarce, pressured, and fleeting.

You start to think (and maybe say out loud) frustrations such as, "I can't find the time to get those tests graded!" or "I don't have the time to get my car washed, or prepare those meals, or get the laundry done, or go for my walk, or pay my bills, or go to the doctor, or write that note to my friend, or find quiet time, or _____."

Yet there is this gradual awareness and understanding that sets into your life when you exercise a high level of self-control throughout the week. You begin to realize time is something you *make*, not something you *find*.

What are your initial thoughts about the phrase, *Time is something you* make, *not something you* find?

_____
_____
_____
_____
_____
_____
_____
_____
_____
_____
_____
_____
_____
_____
_____
_____
_____
_____
_____
_____
_____
_____

MY JOY

My first teaching job was in a small, rural school. I drove a morning school bus route to supplement my salary. I had this very real sense of time based on the expectations for showing up at each bus stop. There was a lot of ground to cover on that bus run, and sometimes I would be late to the stop. I would hear about it from the bus company as they fielded complaints from parents. I remember thinking there just wasn't *enough time provided on the bus schedule* to drive safely and meet those expectations.

Since I was teaching mostly middle school and high school students, my daily life revolved around the timing of our bell schedule. That schedule and those minutes marched on, even when I wasn't quite done with my lesson or finished with that bus run. It felt to me like I was always running to catch up with the schedule.

During my third year of teaching, I finally had the time issue under control. Until I was called into the office by the principal. Since I seemed to be doing so well, he wanted to know if I would be willing to coach in our new fall volleyball program at the school. My first thought was, "How will I *find* the time?"

He indicated I should only say *yes* if I am willing to *make the time* to honor the commitment of taking on the additional task. He gave me twenty-four hours to decide. Could I *make the time* to coach another sport? There would be a tempting stipend.

Finding the time is essentially a dismissive, indefinite action. When you say to someone, "I'll find the time," you are not committing to action. *Making* the time indicates a movement to action and makes it a priority on your calendar.

Knowing time was fixed, I went home that night and wrote out a list of all my current *make-the-time* commitments. Could I cram in more stuff to the fixed time in my days and nights?

The following is the list from my reflection.

1. Teaching five mathematics classes and one health education class: Preparing, grading, communicating with parents, and more.
2. Driving my early-morning school bus route.
3. Meeting weekly with our new grades 6–8 mathematics teacher.
4. Prepping new materials for the revised, state-required health education standards.
5. Coaching winter and spring sports from mid-October through late May.
6. Coaching our newly formed mathematics competition team at the local community college on Monday nights.
7. Playing men's fall softball with my friends on Tuesday and Thursday nights.
8. Teaching a Saturday calculus class at the local community college (for rent money).
9. Sleeping seven hours.
10. Attending a graduate school class on Wednesday nights (on teaching middle school mathematics standards) at the university, which was forty-five miles away.

I was surprised by the extensive nature of my *make-the-time* list. I was left wondering how many commitments on my list were *essential*. Did these commitments bring me joy *and* align with my values? I then decided it was time to take action on my *make-the-time* list!

The next day I went to see the principal and told him *no* to the fall coaching position. I could not *make the time* required. I went to the bus company that afternoon and resigned from my early-morning bus route. I withdrew from my graduate school class and saved it for an action down the road.

There is a link between our perceptions of time and our overall feelings of joy. When we *perceive* that we possess more free time, we tend to report higher levels of joy, as we sense some control over our daily schedule. While the relationship between time and joy is complex, our perceptions about time, how we allocate our time, and our ability to be present in the moment are intertwined when creating the sweet spot of joy.[37]

When you decide to *make the time* for a new activity, you need to decide which activity you will *stop*. Your time decisions should be prioritized based on an alignment with your personal values, interests, and goals each school season. For example, a modern-day, joy-valued list might include the following.

- Daily time with colleagues—teachers, leaders, coaches, counselors, staff members, central office personnel, and more
- Daily time with friends and family members
- Daily time for physical and mental well-being routines
- Daily time for continuous growth for knowledge to improve teaching and learning

The hard truth is that what you *make time* for reveals your identity and priorities.

MY JOY

Make the time to complete this page and determine if your current time commitments are aligned with your values, goals, and priorities in life.

Current Make-the-Time Commitments	Aligned Values, Goals, and Priorities *(Your Why for Each Time Commitment)*

Despite our best efforts to be intentional about our daily joy decisions, sometimes events beyond our control can hijack our joy. Then what? That answer is the subject of the next chapter.

FALL

Hijacked

You define a good flight by negatives: you didn't get hijacked, you didn't crash, you didn't throw up, you weren't late, you weren't nauseated by the food. So you are grateful.
—Paul Theroux

Surprise! What a loaded word.

A *surprise* is an attack made without warning, taking you unawares, or the feeling caused by something unexpected or unusual.[38] Although it is possible you have had some good surprises in your professional and personal life, most likely, you have experienced more than once "the attack without warning" type of surprise at the start of the school season.

Surprises can temporarily knock you off your joy game. No warning.

Consider, for a moment, a few surprising, joy-hijacking moments you may have experienced as the new school year began. Have you experienced any of them? Sustaining joy through the early adjustments can be a challenge.

- *Classroom assignments:* Surprised by class *room* assignments (the location) and class *teaching* assignments, which vary by grade level, subject matter, student population, and available classroom resources.
- *Student assignments:* Surprised by the number of students assigned and student schedule changes one week, one month, or more into the new school year as students move in or out of your classroom.
- *Student needs:* Surprised by the volume of students with diverse learning needs, behavioral challenges, or social-emotional challenges. You do not yet have special education colleagues assigned for daily collaboration, insight, and mutual engagement into student learning.

Write about a start-of-the-school-year moment when your joy was briefly hijacked by surprises or *circumstances outside of your control.*

- *Administrative changes:* Surprised by a new principal. New initiatives or new mandates that require additional time and effort to implement. You feel the pressure to adapt quickly to unfamiliar expectations.
- *Classroom environments:* Surprised by the physical condition of your assigned classroom—maintenance issues, safety concerns, too few desks, and inadequate resources.
- *Workload and time constraints:* Surprised by the request to add an administrative duty to your current assignment. This last-minute request places an additional demand on your workload and extends your day by an hour. Dropping off and picking up children at daily childcare will be an issue. There is no additional stipend either.

MY JOY

My first year of teaching was in that rural school district mentioned in the previous chapter. I accepted the job in May and signed a contract to be the *high school* mathematics teacher. I did not hear back from the school district until one week before the school season was to begin in the third week of August.

I arrived on Monday, August 20. The meeting ended, and the principal asked me into his office. They had to make some summer changes due to construction and other staffing issues. I would be teaching grades 5–12, one mathematics class each for grades 5, 6, 7, and 8; algebra and geometry; one combined class of advanced algebra/pre-calculus; and one health education class. An eight-period day. Seven separate preparations for each day. Three different buildings. Surprise!

To say the least, my joy was hijacked, and I had decisions to make. From my perspective, my first year was set up for failure. On the inside, I was distraught.

∞

Where is joy, then? Well, this is where joy as a *choice* comes in! There is a body of research in neuroscience and psychology that supports the idea of experiencing joy through the neuroplasticity of our brain as it changes and adapts throughout life. Engaging in *positive and joyful* experiences can contribute to the rewiring of neural pathways toward joy, essentially promoting our overall well-being.[39]

In theory, that sounds nice, but it is very hard to do. The secret to overcoming a situation when your joy feels hijacked by surprises through decisions made by someone or some event is to figure out how to reengage your brain and turn that surprise situation into a positive experience. How do you do that? By taking positive action.

The pathway for not allowing others to steal your joy is driven by your engagement in positive social interactions with friends, family members, and all those supporting you on your teaching and leading journey this year. When you engage with others, your brain releases oxytocin. Oxytocin is associated with bonding, trust, and positive social relationships.[40] Positive relationships become the place to recapture your joy (see Fall, Chapter 8: Relationships, page 35, and Summer, Chapter 5: Friendship, page 193).

In that first season of my teaching career, I reached out and took several relational actions to help me survive. I contacted my high school mentor teacher. He sent me weekly materials for my lessons.

I made friends with our science teacher. He needed a roommate. I moved. Five-minute drive to work! I created a group of senior student tutors to help me with an after-school mathematics tutoring program for middle school students. The seniors got a service credit. I got some relief.

I began recruiting freshmen and sophomore students to consider taking a third year of mathematics. My rationale was if more students signed up for mathematics classes, more teachers would be needed, and I could teach fewer preps in the future.

I made friends with the cafeteria workers and convinced them to bring me my lunch each day while I prepared for my afternoon classes. I connected with our school counselor and social worker (one and the same person), and she helped me design my health education lessons and was often a guest teacher. I connected with our other counselor, who played men's softball, and I joined his team for some stress relief.

MY JOY

Dwell on these words: *Neuroplasticity is served by engaging in positive and joyful experiences.*

Describe positive actions you took or have taken to reach out to others and choose joy in moments when surprises occurred that briefly tried to hijack your joy.

_____

There is a perseverance story when you make the joy decision to not allow surprise events or situations beyond your control to steal your joy. Joy is often a result of your perseverance routines. That connection is next!

FALL

Perseverance

Perseverance is not a long race; it is many short races one after the other.

—Walter Elliot

You have a story of perseverance. I am sure of it. You chose this profession, after all. *Perseverance* is the "continued effort to do or achieve something despite difficulties, failure, or opposition."[41] That sounds like our job description! I have yet to experience a fall season in which adversity of some kind, at work or at home, did not eventually appear. After all, winter is around the corner.

MY JOY

Perseverance is a long-term mental-wellness response—developed over time—to adverse events in your work and home life (see Winter, Chapter 9: Pause, page 99, for suggestions about short-term responses to adverse moments).

Perseverance as a skill navigates the challenges and setbacks of your work life and empowers you to embrace adversity, overcome obstacles, and keep moving forward. The result is a deep-seated sense of efficacy—the confidence and competence that can often bring profound joy.

Write about a recent moment during the start of this school year that required perseverance in your professional life.

_____
_____
_____
_____
_____
_____
_____
_____
_____
_____
_____
_____
_____
_____
_____
_____

When we experience a moderate level of adversity, better mental health and well-being and higher satisfaction with life are the results.[42] It is through perseverance that we experience joy—not as something fleeting, but as a steadfast companion on our journey. The good news is we can use specific routines and strategies to develop our perseverance skills.

- *Increase self-compassion:* When you increase awareness of your suffering, you are more likely to relieve that suffering because you have experienced similar adversity when helping others (or yourself) through prior obstacles and challenges (see Winter, Chapter 5: Suffering, page 81, and Winter, Chapter 6: Compassion, page 87).
- *Build in self-efficacy:* Your *confidence* and *competence* to overcome adversity increases as you experience adversity. In our cyclical and seasonal profession, the adverse events you experience are not always a surprise to you as you build your skills and confidence to work through past adverse situations with students, parents, and colleagues.
- *Reframe as self-challenges:* When you experience adversity, you can reframe it toward a *challenge* response. This, in turn, gives you additional energy and an increase in adrenaline toward overcoming the obstacle. You feel focused and not fearful. You release a different ratio of stress hormones to access mental and physical resources.[43]

Thus, perseverance routines are enhanced when you consider adversity more like a challenge and less like a threat. You harness a *challenge response* to adversity by asking yourself the following.

- Where do I have control or influence in the situation?
- What are my strengths? And how can I use them to overcome the obstacle?
- What human resources do I have? And how can I ask for and use support from others?
- How do I know I can handle the situation? What are my past experiences? How can my self-care and physical-wellness strategies help me process adversity and persevere?
- What is one specific action step toward resolution I can take *now*?
- How can I break down the adverse situation into small victories, one day at a time?

Perseverance doesn't always look pretty—some days, it's just about muddling through.

The Chicago Marathon was the second weekend in October. Taped up and ready to go at 4:30 a.m., I started the two-mile walk to the corral stations for the race. I could walk with limited pain. So far, so good. My body and my brain were telling me, "Don't run; you are an idiot." My heart was saying, "You have to."

And so, I did. Starting the race was at least something I could control. The pain, however, was not. It was unbearable. So, I said quietly under my breath, "I'll go one mile. That is an action I can take. A small victory. If it keeps getting worse, I'll stop." I also said, "If the pain stays like this, I'll keep going."

This may sound insane, but giving up on that moment because of an injury two weeks prior, after six months of training, seemed impossible to me. Persevering through the race *was* my joy. I knew my body well enough to reframe the race as a challenge.

About one mile in, a "runner's high" kicks in, and dopamine is released as you start to feel energy and a bit of euphoria.[44] Thus, the pain was ever present, but it seemed controllable to me. So, I headed off to mile two. By mile eleven, I was in a groove and settled into a slight limp and at a slower pace. My human resource was my mental strength.

Eventually, I noticed something wrong with my gait. I could no longer feel my left foot touching the ground. My calf had given up. My left foot had gone completely numb. I was at mile twenty-one. More adversity. More perseverance required. There was a first-aid station at mile twenty-two. I asked for support. I had them put a numbing spray on both my legs, especially my left calf and quad, a double dose. I started off again. Another small victory.

At mile twenty-five, my left leg finally screamed, "No more!" It had rightfully given up on me. So, I started to sing quietly and eventually a little bit louder—*the Chicago Bears' fight song*. Over and over and over. This song served as my strength. You might wonder why.

I was running for Alzheimer's that day. My *naz* friend (see Summer, Chapter 6: *Naz*, page 197) of thirty years had died of the devasting disease. He did not know me near the end of his life. Whatever momentary physical pain I was experiencing could not compare to the pain that had resided inside of him. I was doing this for both of us. My purpose, my *why*, far surpassed my obstacle. That stupid fight song brought me joy—joy that was found in allowing myself to exist inside the memories of our best times together.

Just as I had imagined it, I made it to the sign that said *400 yards to go*. I went as fast as I could. Sprinting all the way, although video review would show I was barely moving. Dragging my leg across that finish line. I looked up and thanked God for getting me through to the end, for my family, my friends, and the more than two hundred people who donated to the Alzheimer's charity in memory of my best friend.

Joy moments of perseverance are like that.

My story is about overcoming adversity through perseverance. Most of you reading this are not runners. However, I know you have persevered or are persevering through whatever hardship, adversity, or obstacle you currently face during the fall season or any part of your school-year life.

Whatever you do, don't give up. *Know in your heart* that our profession needs *you*.

MY JOY

What is your story of perseverance? What is something hard you are persevering through right now? Provide some detail on how your perseverance is supporting your joy journey this school year. And, if appropriate, share with a trusted friend.

_____
_____
_____
_____
_____
_____
_____
_____
_____
_____
_____
_____

This race was run near the end of the fall season. The seasons have beginnings and endings too. Thanksgiving is now upon us. Fall season is ending. Joy waits for you.

FALL

We must find time to stop and thank the people who make a difference in our lives.

—John F. Kennedy

Dear reader: I am writing this final chapter in part 1 different from the others. It is written as a dialogue between me and you as we approach the end of the fall season. Your voice is in italics. Enjoy!

Thanksgiving

The date is arriving. Another Thanksgiving is closing in quickly.

I know, time waits for no one! It has been relentless.

A third of this school year is in your rearview mirror now. Congrats.

Thanks. I need the Thanksgiving "time out" right about now.

When the date arrives, the colors of autumn will mostly be gone.

Agreed. Where I live, the grass is turning brown, and the leaves are down. Feels like nature is signaling an ending.

Daylight is fading. Gray skies, strong winds, more rain, and occasional light snowstorms await.

I can feel it too. Where are my winter coats?

They will be at your table this weekend.

Wait. What?

Your family and friends—your old comfortable coats. They will show up at your table.

I get what you are saying. We share, laugh, tell stories, cry, and hope. The old coats that are my family and friends, right?

Yes. It's as if you were never apart, despite the distance and time. You learn to live comfortably with those old coats. They eventually assume your wrinkles, do not hurt you anywhere, mold to your deformities. You feel their presence because they keep you warm.[45]

Who said that?

Victor Hugo.

What does he know about it?

A lot, I think. Those friends and family members keep your life full and imperfect and alive. You miss them when they are not in the room at the table.

Will the old coats be at my table next year?

There are no guarantees.

I pray for it silently and softly, "Is this the last time these coats will be worn by me?"

There is a settled sadness in not knowing.

I have felt that sadness before. A disjointed dissonance when the old coats are gone.

Yes. We secretly fear we may be the ones no longer at the future Thanksgiving table.

That thought is too painful to bear.

This Thanksgiving, promise that, wherever your table may be, you will be brave enough to savor the moment, connect with others more deeply, and cultivate joy. Tell them *thanks*.

That will relieve some of my future worry and pain?

Absolutely!

OK. I will reach out and let my old coats know how much I love them, how much they matter, and celebrate their presence at my table.

That is the point of making time for Thanksgiving. The true joy.

Should I tell them or write it to them?

Yes. Both. Often.

Happy Thanksgiving, old coats!

MY JOY

When you have a quiet moment, write about the old coats in your life—the ones that love you despite your deformities, as Victor Hugo reminds us. Send them a note of thanks. Don't delay!

Fall:
A Season to Renew
Your Conclusions

During this fall season, which of the joy actions in Fall chapters 1–13 most resonated with your current personal and professional joy journey—a school season of new beginnings? In reflection, what are three to five brief takeaways about growing strong during a season of new beginnings?

--- **MY** J O Y ♥ ---

Write about some of your favorite takeaways from this fall season that might serve your overall joy journey as an educator and your well-being as you begin the heavy lifting ahead during the winter months. How did you do with your joy journey this past fall season?

_____
_____
_____
_____
_____
_____
_____

You can check out my video here, where I provide my conclusions and insights from Part 1: Fall—A Season to Renew. Thanks for joining the fall journey with me. It was fun!

PART 2

WINTER:
A SEASON TO BE RESOLUTE

Growing Strong in a Season of Heavy Lifting

What good is the warmth of summer, without the cold of winter to give it sweetness?

—John Steinbeck

Winter is a season of resilience. Winter presents a season of resoluteness with the challenge of physical, mental, and emotional weariness. The weather shifts, and you wind your way through holidays. One semester ends and a new one waits to begin. It is the midlife of the school year, and the ending of your school-year story seems too far off to touch. Can you sustain a high level of positive emotional energy, joy, and inspiration for your students and colleagues during the grind of winter? You might make it through the December holidays with your joy intact, yet the January and February months are waiting to drag you down. Resoluteness is required as you solve problems unique to winter weather and the winter school months ahead. *Once again.*

The winter months are filled with expectations met *and* expectations that can leave you disappointed. Weather shifts can provide beautiful snowy landscapes *and* icy shadows of dark ice with frigid temperatures and harsh winds. Heavier coats. Hats, gloves, and scarves. Frost-bitten fingers. Colder days. Rainier days. Shorter daylight hours. Darkness to and from school. The disappointing and discouraging list runs long.

Creating a warm, positive, and inviting classroom climate can offset the heavy lifting of those dark winter months. Resoluteness required. The chapters for this season of your school life are designed to help you stay connected to life's joy and the best parts of the winter school season by using effective mindfulness routines. The best version of you. Every day. Resilience required.

Thus, Winter chapters 1–13 provide helpful strategies for showing up daily and sustaining *chronic* joy despite the adversity that is sure to catch you by surprise. Use and enjoy the mental- and emotional-wellness strategies, such as *silence* in chapter 3 (page 71), the *suffering-compassion* combination of chapters 5 and 6 (pages 81 and 87), the *worry-gezellig* connections of chapters 7 and 8 (pages 91 and 95), and the *pause-balance* pairing of chapters 9 and 10 (pages 99 and 103). I hope you enjoy these two-part chapter combinations. By the way, *gezellig* has become one of my favorite new words!

Yes, you can remain the kind of educator who presents an authentic and positive emotional state during the most difficult winter school seasons—cold-, snow-, or rain-filled gray skies and darker days. You just need to remain resolute!

WINTER

Resolute

Winter is not a season, it's a celebration.

—Anamika Mishra

"Help wanted: Resolute persons required."

As December begins and winter arrives, we find ourselves confronted with the inevitable challenges and hardships that accompany the winter season of our professional life. We head to work as the days get colder, icier, and darker during the drive from and to home.

During my twentieth season as a teacher in the suburban Chicago prairie, our east-campus faculty parking lot got moved to a smaller space on the south side of the school. As the winter season closed in, the north winds whipped around our cars and froze our windshields and side mirrors. My driver's-side door did not completely close, and the snow and ice ended up inside my car. The walk to the building entrance was about two hundred yards. *Hardiness required!*

I would intentionally arrive early so I could park my car facing southeast. That way, the winds, ice, or snow would do minimal harm. I carried a pair of jumper cables in my car in case I needed a cold battery start or my colleagues needed to jumpstart their cars in the late afternoon. *Scrapers required!*

Yet, it was the walk to the building that always got the best of me. My eyes would start to water, and icicles would form on my mustache and beard. You had to walk bent at a forty-five-degree angle at the waist and lean into those winds to make it to the safety of the building.

Are you a resolute person? What's something you did recently that reflected a resolute mindset at work or at home?

_____
_____
_____
_____
_____
_____
_____
_____
_____
_____
_____
_____
_____
_____
_____
_____
_____
_____
_____
_____
_____

Mondays were always the most difficult, as the heat ramped up from the weekend building shutdown. *Heavy coats required!*

The school year was aging now. We were almost halfway to the end of the school year. Every aspect of our work and home life just felt more stress-filled and demanding than at the beginning of the school year—way, way back in August.

December has this triple whammy in a way—the end of a semester drawing near, winter's fierceness fast approaching, parent conferences planned, report cards due, and the stress of expectations (met and unmet) with various holidays ahead. These forces collide as winter begins and the calendar year ends. Conceding power to the dynamics of these forces can be dangerous to our daily well-being and joy.

A loss of *resilience* (defined as positive adaptation despite adversity) is inevitable with the winter season settling in.[46] We fight through the inclination to lose our resilience and check out mentally, physically, and emotionally.

Resolute persons required, indeed!

So, what does *resolute* mean, exactly?

It means you demonstrate determination as you lean into those strong winds of winter. You demonstrate an unwavering commitment to pursuing your goals for student learning (see Fall, Chapter 7: Yearning, page 31). You remind yourself *daily* to stay connected to the same strong sense of purpose you possessed at the start of the fall season. You *show up* each day with a resilience in the face of the increased challenges and adversity posed by the weather condition's collision with December events and expectations.

MY JOY

You are characterized by others as steadfast, persevering, and willing to stay focused on student learning. You maintain a positive emotional outlook by choosing your most positive emotional presence every day.[47]

You have an unwavering resolve to move toward *finishing* December and the eventual school semester *well*.

Resolute persons can create joy by moving *toward* habituation to minimize stressors.

Recall our joy discussion in Fall, Chapter 9: Habituation (page 39). We examined the secret to *fighting off* stagnation by moving *away* from habituation. When we habituate, "we respond less and less to stimuli that repeat."[48]

However, there is also an upside to *restoring* habituation to help overcome winter season stressors. Moving toward habituation adds structure to the chaos of increased stress. Holding steadfast to your routines in winter can lead to less stress and increased time for creativity and innovative thinking as the long march of the winter season begins.

What are some daily habituation routines that can help you remain resolute and steadfast in your work life as December begins?

- *Seek self-care:* Schedule regular breaks away from the noise of work and social media. Engage in activities that rejuvenate you. Maybe a workout or a walk outside while dressed appropriately for the weather. Pay attention to your emotional well-being by acknowledging and participating in moments of genuine laughter with a trusted colleague during the toughest days.
- *Seek celebration:* Have parties in December, both at work and at home! Acknowledge and celebrate your achievements, big and small. Recognize progress, milestones, and contributions to student learning and well-being with your colleagues and friends. Celebrating weekly successes before you leave for the winter holiday can boost your morale and reinforce a shared sense of purpose with colleagues from the start of the school year.
- *Seek out joy:* Look more closely at students, colleagues, and family members. They are entering winter too. Who among them is inspiring you these days? Whether witnessing a student's breakthrough, connecting with colleagues, engaging in creative teaching strategies, or preparing for the holiday with family members, look for opportunities to thank them and infuse joy into their work, world, and effort. Helping others during their holiday struggle is a way to fuel and feed your joy. Look beyond your*self* and inspire others.

Resoluteness. Resilience. Determination.

Get your coats and armor on. Winter is coming, and it wants to defeat you. Don't let it. Stay resolute in pursuit of *your* joy. It will empower you to find fulfillment amid the ebb and flow of your daily circumstances. Cultivate resilience in those around you. Encourage them. Also, maintain and seek support from others; this allows them to be more resolute too. You can do it!

MY JOY

Take a close look at the three strategies for maintaining joy in the face of winter. Which strategy most resonates with you? How will you take action to stand resolute and move toward joy before winter break?

___

Being resolute in your joy search during the winter months can be difficult to do. The hardships are real. They require a bigger type of joy experience. *Chronic joy*. And that experience is next!

WINTER

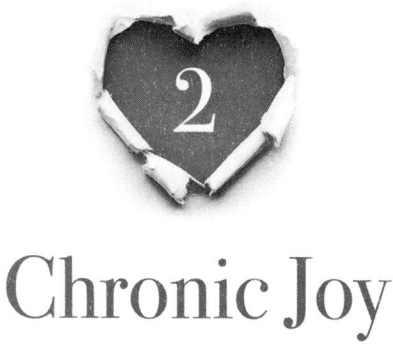

Chronic Joy

Optimism is a form of rebellion.
—Cornel West

It was during the winter season; I wanted to give up.

Physically, mentally, and emotionally, I was a mess. Seven months prior, I had major heart surgery. It was my thirtieth season as a teacher. Now, the electrical rhythms of my heart were skipping out of control, with a resting heart rate consistently near 140 beats per minute. The current weekly solution was to leave my teaching job in my school district (by then, I was the superintendent) on Tuesdays, walk into the emergency room of the local hospital with a suit on, have them knock me out, and "put the paddles" on me. Essentially, they would shock my heart back into a normal rhythm. If I was lucky, it might last a week.

It never did.

Like every educator, the daily demands of my job did not care that I was experiencing a general energy malaise I had to fight through each day to be the kind of high-energy teacher and leader those around me needed and expected from me. My home life was intense as well, and the one close friend I could share my frustrations, fears, and concerns with was experiencing health issues far worse than mine. So, I suffered in silence. I had this chronic heart issue that various medical solutions offered to fix but none could *resolve*.

Winter is a season that needs our *resolve*. To choose joy, again and again, including every Tuesday in the emergency room.

Do you believe you have a general daily resolve and disposition to move toward joy? Why or why not?

_____
_____
_____
_____
_____
_____
_____
_____
_____
_____
_____
_____
_____
_____
_____
_____
_____
_____
_____
_____

To say the least, I was in a steady state of unhappiness. My daily experiences were difficult at best. And yet, what sustained me during this ongoing saga was a general disposition, a resolve, toward joy. I am not entirely sure of the source for that disposition.

Was it inherited from my parents? *I don't think so.*

Was it based on a role model in my life? *Maybe.*

Was it something I just said one day? "I'll choose joy." *Not that I can recall.*

Was it steeped in my faith? *Hard to tell.*

MY JOY

As mentioned in the introduction (page 1), research confirms that about 40 percent of our disposition toward joy is genetic, and the other 60 percent can be developed.[49] From the moment I began my teaching career, I had this vague awareness that *my joy* was the one thing I could control (the 60 percent, I suppose). No one could steal it away from me. Most of my teaching life, I have encountered so many events, rules, regulations, stressors, and experiences that I do not control. Joy, however, was something I could *choose*, or not.

How do we choose joy?, you might wonder.

Joy is so much more than a feeling. Joy is an *acknowledgment* of your surroundings, of your friends, and family, the messiness, the beauty, and sometimes the grief of life. And that acknowledgment frees you up to see the beauty in most moments, on most days.

The paddles that shocked my heart left me a bit bruised and hazy when I regained consciousness. It was not a happy feeling. And yet, after the required thirty minutes of observation, the hospital would release me, and I would drive home on a crisp and cold Chicago winter evening. Surprisingly, I would be amazed by the vibrant colors of the sun setting against a darkening sky. I could feel it, sense it. Smell it. Taste it. I would pull the car into the parking lot of a grocery store or a park near the hospital, get out of my car, and just revel in the taste and smell of the crisp air, the trails of colored light left from the sunset, and the feeling of being alive (see Fall, Chapter 5: Nature, page 23, and Winter, Chapter 6: Compassion, page 87).

Sounds strange, right?

I was experiencing something called *chronic joy*. The simple act of seeing the sunset and the colors in the early-evening sky and smelling the cool, crisp air provided a dopamine release. Dopamine is a neurotransmitter associated with pleasure and reward. Simple, enjoyable activities can trigger the release of dopamine in the brain, reinforcing positive feelings and encouraging a sense of joy.[50]

Sometimes, depending on my overall mood, I would just stand in the quiet. Sometimes, I would play a song that allowed good memories to lighten my load. *Chronic joy.*

What a paradox. The word *chronic* is usually associated with a problem, like chronic heart problems. Chronic as in *something continuing or occurring again and again for a long time.*

Chronic joy. Joy continuing again, and again, and again, for a long time. Like an entire school year? Yes. Our entire lives. Is it possible? Yes. We can be educators, family members, parents, and human beings that experience suffering, yet live a life of chronic joy.

I believe chronic joy, then, is the experience of joy as a consistent and ongoing aspect of your life. A general and genuine positive outlook with a disposition toward engaging in actions and activities that elicit joy in you and in others.

Be aware that chronic joy is not constant happiness, which is both unrealistic and unsustainable. What chronic joy is, however, is a *resilience*, a resoluteness, that allows you to experience joy amid life's challenging moments and circumstances.

Winter is a season of resilience. Make the move now. Chronic joy awaits. Even if you are struggling in the hardship of this winter day.

MY JOY

Joy is an acknowledgment of your surroundings, your friends, your family, the messiness, the beauty, and sometimes the grief of life. Chronic joy is the experience of joy as a consistent and ongoing aspect of your life.

Write an acknowledgment of the circumstances, surroundings, family, and friends in your life. Describe a specific time when you were resolved to be more aware of acknowledging and choosing the pursuit of chronic joy, despite difficult circumstances.

Silence is intertwined with the essence of sustaining chronic joy. That connection is next!

WINTER

Silence

In the stillness of the mind, I saw myself as I am: unbound.
—Nisargadatta Maharaj

Silence has the power to amplify the experience of joy.

Just think about it. Oh, that's right; you can't hear yourself think. The daily noises of school life, social media, and the loud and soft voices speaking at and around you are deafening.

There. Is. No. Silence.

And yet, winter offers up some incredible moments of joy-filled quietude (silence and quiet), if we just *make the time* for them. There can be a tranquil nature to winter's serenity and stillness. The crisp air, the blanket of snow, the bare branches of trees with patterns etched in frost and ice.

There are moments during winter mornings or late winter evenings when the world seems to pause, if you just take a walk outside. There is a profound beauty to be found—a beauty that speaks in the gentle embrace of the silence. You can see and hear your breath. You immerse yourself in the gift of that stillness. And, it is in that moment, away from the grind of daily life, that you find joy at a much deeper level, offering up a resilience for the day ahead, today or perhaps tomorrow.

Do you know this kind of peace and joy? Joy in the silence?

Describe a time when you experienced the silence of winter and were grateful for the silence and quiet it offered. What did you see and hear?

_____
_____
_____
_____
_____
_____
_____
_____
_____
_____
_____
_____
_____
_____
_____
_____
_____
_____
_____
_____
_____
_____

MY JOY

There has always been a bit of magic in the air (for me, at least) with the winter and the holiday season. Despite the season being one of natural celebrations with colleagues, students, family, and friends, I have balanced those expectations by enjoying intentional quiet walks in the early winter evening, alone.

Those walks are about the deep and silent moments that transcend the day-to-day grind and the work we do. During my forty-ninth season—I sometimes felt the weight of those seasons stacking on top of me—I was working at a December institute for preK–12 teachers and leaders in Colorado.

Prior to the institute, my travel and speaking schedule had been crushing. Like some of my seasons as a teacher and coach, there had been no time to take a break from the intensity and relentless nature of my work and home life. There was no time to prepare for the stress of the holidays. Taking the time to stand or sit in silence, letting my brain process all that was going on around me, seemed like a waste. Yet, when I sense my life drifting away from things that really matter, and I start feeling overwhelmed, I know it is time for some silence.

So, at 5:10 p.m., at the end of a three-day teaching event, I headed out for a much-needed run at dusk. It is that thirty minutes or so of twilight when you can often feel the power of something bigger than you. I *needed* that run... nice and easy.

I used my AllTrails app to find a place to run. Perfect! Five-mile trip in the cold, crisp air; light snow on the ground; and 41 degrees Fahrenheit at 5,500 feet elevation. It was getting a bit colder as the sun disappeared with low winds. I bundled up, put on some gloves, and followed my map directions out the door.

The first mile and a half took me through a wilderness area that was *deeply* quiet. What a gift to get away from the noise and exhaustive energy of the past month. Then, the trail took me past fenced-in backyards and the parks of a few neighborhoods. I was running along a wide path between the backyards of a long row of homes. By now, it was dark, and lights from those houses lit up the area around me. The beauty of it all warmed me. All I could hear was my breathing, and I could feel the fresh air as my brain started to clear from the noise and clutter of my day. My week, really.

The path was an out and back, and the only night-sky light came from the crystal-clear stars above me. I hit that wilderness spot on my return, and the depth of the dark and the quiet was beyond anything I had ever experienced.

Now that it was dark, I could tell I was up on a ridge. In the clear winter night, I could see for miles—the outline of lights from homes in the distance—the stars and the long trail of car headlights from workers heading home. Down below, where the path was about to take me, it was completely dark.

As I descended the path to the bottom, I was overwhelmed by this solitary, silent moment. The silence was deafening. I stopped, sat on a nearby bench, and reveled in the moment. There was a joy in that exact moment that is hard to explain. I had slowed down my brain long enough to *be* in this deep moment of quiet. I *acknowledged* my life was worth *something*. Just maybe, my presence as a father, husband, friend, and teacher was making a small but meaningful difference to some people. And, in that very moment, in the dark of the night at about 6:05 p.m., I could feel my worth as a human being. There were quiet tears of joy. It felt oddly humbling. It is a memory I keep in my pocket and bring out during more difficult moments of my life. When other worldly forces speak to me differently.

I stood up a bit stiffly and walked forward, realizing my body was getting cold and feeling a bit old too. I put my gloves back on and started a slow jog along the path in the ravine. As I reflected on the moment, I knew in my heart that none of my work as an educator had happened without the shoulders of others to stand on. The true blessing of a few great mentors.

I finished my jog and walked a bit more to cool down, thinking about the people in my life who were not beside me anymore and how much I deeply missed them. I gave thanks for their impact on me. I then gave thanks for the family and friends in my life who walk with me still and love me enough—warts and all.

I was reminded that despite all the winter hardship in the world, from time to time—even on a suburban ridge in Colorado—I can find my worth if I just open the door to the silence. And, to my spiritual self.

Amid the winter harshness, there is a beauty that speaks not in words, but in gentle silence. My hope for you is that you will occasionally immerse yourself in the joy that comes from the stillness and peace that winter brings. How silence is achieved is unique to each of us. It may not be out on an early evening run. Time and place do not matter as much as the intentionality and commitment to it.

Choose what works best for you and remember, silence is a gift to yourself. Without silent moments, it will be difficult to achieve the life balance (shared ahead in Winter, Chapter 8: *Gezellig*, page 95) we so desperately need to be relationally successful at work and at home.

MY JOY

Use the winter season to acknowledge your worth and renew your purpose. Take time to sit, stand, walk, or run into the silence. How will you give yourself this gift?

_____
_____
_____
_____
_____
_____
_____

Write about your experiences with silence and what works best for you.

_____
_____
_____
_____
_____
_____
_____

By linking your New Year's Eve resolutions to the pursuit of joy discussed thus far, you set the stage for establishing new habits and routines that can propel you toward personal-wellness goals. That connection to joy is next!

WINTER

Comparison

Comparison is the thief of joy.
—Theodore Roosevelt, Jr.

The post-holiday winter of my twenty-sixth season as a teacher.

I walked out of the gym where I exercised after school three days a week. As I walked to my car in the well-lit parking lot, I was proofreading some pages from a project and not really paying much attention to myself or my surroundings. I had a vague awareness that my non-gloved hand, the one holding the papers, was extremely cold.

The walk included a narrow bridge over a small ditch. As I crossed the bridge, I hit a patch of black ice, fell flat on my back, and rolled into the shallow ditch. My backpack softened the blow, my papers went flying, and my wrist took the brunt of the fall. I popped right back up, climbed out of the ditch, and looked around to see if anyone noticed my awkward fall. I was a bit embarrassed and glad no one was around. My papers were spread all over the place, but physically everything seemed to check out OK.

I drove the twenty-six-mile trek home, which in the winter took double the usual time required. Parking in the street—my driveway needed to be shoveled, of course—I got out of my car and noticed pain in my right knee. A lot more pain than in my wrist.

Shortly after that fall, follow-up doctor visits resulted in physical therapy. Although I did not know it at the time, the knee injury (a partially torn ligament) was the beginning of my decision to stop any form of movement.

I just stopped. *I rationalized.* I needed time to recover. It would be a relief to no longer add working out to my busy list of home, work, and longer-than-normal commute times. My busy winter life included coaching my own children; going to graduate school; working on a new book; and making time for my family, friends, and faith.

My health-related issues started with a decision to stop moving. I was surprised by how good it felt to *not* maintain a movement routine. My days were busy enough. I rationalized, "After all, my knee needs time to recover!"

By the winter of my *twenty-seventh season* of teaching, my knee was fully recovered, but I still ignored most movement activities. Again, I rationalized. My body needed a break. There were a few times I vowed to start intentionally moving again on the first day of the next month. That date would always come and go. Still no movement.

Everything around me was ramping up in intensity. I was moving toward a different job with more responsibility. I was deeper now into the demands of my dissertation work and trying to balance the responsibilities of family and home. To make my physical-wellness situation worse, I was eating on the run and cutting corners on my sleep—less than five hours per night—and most dinner meals were fast food for my fast-paced life. I just had other priorities. *I rationalized* some more. I understood intellectually the need to get a grip on my physical health, but the road was too long. I just couldn't get started again.

By the winter of my *twenty-eighth season,* I had completely abandoned all pretense of movement activities. Outdoor activities, such as sledding down a local hill with the kids, had become a chore for me. This time, my rationalization was easy: "I'll never look like *that!*"

And *that* referred to the pictures of me from three winters ago before I fell. It also referenced many of my colleagues, friends, and family members with their positive physical health dispositions and appearances. "I'll never be as good as them," I thought.

Here is the problem with that mantra. No matter what we do, there will always be someone somewhere who is bigger than, better than, stronger than, faster than, smarter than, wiser than, better looking than, a better driver than, a better climber than, a better friend than . . . well, you get the point.

Comparison is, indeed, the thief of our joy.

And then, the summer before my *twenty-ninth season* as a teacher and school leader, my body said, "Enough." As I chronicled in *HEART!*, I ended up in a hospital with a heart attack.[51] It got my attention. I stopped all rationalizations, and for the first time in quite a while, my physical wellness became my intentional daily mission, and I found joy in micro improvements. I began comparing myself to the only other person that matters in the comparison game: *me*.

I challenged myself to answer the following three movement questions.

1. What movement activity do I most enjoy?
2. Do I like how it makes me *feel*? (Is there joy?)
3. Can I fit the activity into the flow of my normal workday? (*Make the time.*)

Based on my answers, I set short- and long-term running goals, in my case, my movement of choice (it may not be yours). Long term, I decided to run in a marathon again. That goal took twenty years! Short term, I decided to put on my running clothes, shoes, and socks and sit out on the curb—for two minutes. Eventually, I set the goal of walking two blocks, and then five blocks, and then one mile. Small increments where I compared my physical wellness self-improvement to . . . myself.

I did not know it at the time, but I was following the advice of James Clear regarding how to build atomic habits that stick as you stretch to hold onto and then achieve action toward those New Year's resolutions you set as the new calendar year began.[52]

From Clear's perspective, sustaining a new habit or routine involves several key principles that are rooted in the science of behavior change. Clear emphasizes

Describe an aspect of your life in which comparing yourself to others feels like an uphill battle of futility.

_____
_____
_____
_____
_____
_____
_____
_____
_____
_____
_____
_____
_____
_____
_____
_____
_____
_____
_____
_____
_____
_____
_____
_____
_____
_____
_____

the importance of starting small and making incremental progress. By breaking down a desired habit into manageable, bite-sized actions, you can build momentum and establish a positive feedback loop for success.[53] This is why starting out small, post–heart attack, and gradually increasing my pace and distances created a new routine that once again became a lifetime habit toward joy.

As I write this chapter, I am still standing. That alone is a big deal! I do not take one day of it for granted. And neither should you. You don't need to have a heart attack to sit up and pay attention to sustaining those New Year's resolution habits well past winter and experiencing the quiet joy of long-term physical-wellness success.

MY JOY

Consider your movement routines that help balance your life during winter. Answer the five questions as best you can and share with a trusted friend.

What is the movement activity I most enjoy?

How does it make me *feel*? (Is there joy?)

Can I fit the activity into the flow of my normal workday?

What is a short-term, five-minute activity I could do each day to get started?

What is my long-term action or movement goal for eighteen months from now?

Suffering, it turns out, is not for comparison with others. Suffering, and more importantly, your response to suffering, is connected to joy. Those *two chapters* are next.

WINTER

Suffering

Out of suffering have emerged the strongest souls; the most massive characters are seared with scars.

—Kahlil Gibran

These next two chapters represent a two-part joy episode. Suffering (this chapter) and Compassion (chapter 6, page 87) go hand in hand, or they don't go at all. I hope you can find some joy and solace in the words that follow.

Winter is rolling along. Winter can have its picturesque charm, yet winter's unforgiving nature can also test your resilience and your patience. The winter season can quickly become *insufferable*—as in, *intolerable* or not to be endured.[54] And we share the scars of past winters to prove it!

Winter has a biting cold with relentless rain and snowstorms, icy roads with increased risk of accidents on our way to and from work, commutes that take longer, and salt cemented to our cars that can't be washed off without freezing doors shut. An edginess sets in. We come home to shoveling heavy, wet snow, almost too tired to clear room for our car in a parking lot, street, or possibly, a garage. There are family seasonal illnesses that hit one of us and then all of us.

The frigid temperatures and limited daylight hours also take a toll on our mental well-being, contributing to feelings of lethargy, isolation, irritability, frustration, and seasonal affective disorder.[55] Furthermore, the need for extra layers of clothing and the constant battle against dry skin, chapped lips, or frozen fingers and toes add to your daily inconveniences.

What is a personal story about an experience of *winter suffering*?

_____
_____
_____
_____
_____
_____
_____
_____
_____
_____
_____
_____
_____
_____
_____
_____
_____
_____
_____
_____
_____
_____
_____
_____
_____
_____

Winter. Love it. And hate it. Awe-inspiring *and* suffering-inducing. The good and the difficult. Winter offers up the gift of pain as it amplifies our awareness that students and colleagues are suffering too.

Pain and suffering are a *gift*? It's counterintuitive, but yes.

We don't seek out pain and suffering willingly, yet winter brings it on anyway. Tragedy, sadness, and failure come. Resilience is the residence where our character is forged based on our response choices. Lean in and embrace winter or lean away and hide from it. Your choice. Your decision.

Fortifying ourselves against the realities of winter is achieved by being more honest, talking more deeply about the layers of our daily life experiences, and strengthening our minds and bodies for the inevitable hardships that are part of life—not just part of our winter life. Our "greatness comes from character. And character isn't formed out of smart people, it's formed out of people who suffered."[56]

Using this logic, winter is outdoing itself in trying to build and shape my character development this year! It can stop now. I think I'm good to go.

MY JOY

In January of my thirteenth season as a teacher, I had the benefit of being part of the faculty and staff interview and hiring committee for our new principal. We began working on the questions to ask each candidate. As a committee, we had agreed to focus priorities on the three Cs: character, competence, and commitment (to our school values).

We agreed that, in the end, character (emotional intelligence) was to be first and foremost. It is everything. It can't be hidden, and it can't be compensated for. Our professional learning community needed to be led by a principal who had the mental, emotional, and social skills necessary to lead our faculty and staff. With character first in mind, I mentioned to the committee one question I personally wanted to ask each candidate.

Tell us about a time of pain and suffering (big or small) in your personal or professional life that you are willing to share. How did you respond to that moment in your life?

This can be a difficult question to answer. *Suffering* means to submit to or be forced to endure.[57] Similar to how we learn to *endure* the heavy lifting of the winter months of a school season. While suffering is inherently an unpleasant experience, it also serves as a catalyst for building our resilience and empathy.

The road to self-empathy is paved through the *acknowledgment* of our suffering and then making the decision to emotionally connect to it. When you experience self-empathy, the pain centers in your brain light up—the same pain centers that light up when you stub your toe.[58] Ouch.

Enduring winter's hardships strengthens your character by fostering qualities such as perseverance, courage, and adaptability. We adapt despite the inconveniences and "pains" endured daily. It is through that adaptation that our *response* to pain and suffering (see Winter, Chapter 6: Compassion, page 87) develops the character of who we are today when we interact with others.

I mentioned to the hiring committee that the "pain and suffering" question would help us understand how each principal candidate responds to the inevitable adversity and hardships of a school season. How would each candidate describe their pathway for overcoming obstacles, challenges, and the sustained suffering of student and adult achievement and growth?

I posited that we just might uncover their inner strength and capability for cultivating an empathetic and compassionate school culture for our students, teachers, and community. Would the candidate have the capacity to support and uplift us during the adversity we would surely endure in the next school year?

My hope was that, as the principal candidates described their stories to us, we would hear phrases like:

Don't disconnect from suffering. Acknowledge it. Talk about it. Write about it. Act on it.

We might also learn from each candidate how we (teachers, counselors, administrators, and support staff) could respond to the emotional suffering that creeps into our lives.

When you moderate your reaction to negative events or difficulties, "you demonstrate fewer extreme reactions, less negative emotions, more accepting thoughts, and a greater tendency to put [your] problems into perspective. And, at the same time acknowledge [your] own responsibility to own your daily emotional wellness."[59]

In Fall, Chapter 8: Relationships (page 35), I discussed how the worst joy decision we can make is to go at it alone. Suffering is that way too. It is not something we should do alone, at least not for very long. I know this firsthand. I have tried to go at it alone during some of my deepest moments of suffering and pain, and it has always failed. In some ways, my decision to go at it alone pushed away people that loved me.

Great relationships, deeper relationships, are born and forged out of admitting to painful events, mistakes, or suffering situations. Encourage your trusted friends to be there for you and for each other. Help them find the good in the bad times and talk through the tough and very real stuff of life. Joy resides in those moments and those places where we share our journey and trials with trusted others.

As educators, we are not exempt from suffering. Nor should we want to be. There are many moments in our professional and personal life journeys, both hidden and public, that can cause suffering, difficulty, and conscious endurance.

In this chapter's epigraph, Kahlil Gibran tells us, "Out of suffering have emerged the strongest souls; the most massive characters are seared with scars."[60]

Write a story from your life when you shared your suffering with a friend. How did it strengthen the relationship? How did it help heal your scars?

_____
_____
_____
_____
_____
_____
_____
_____
_____

To suffer deeply means to be wounded at the story level of life—to be "seared with scars," as you read in the epigraph. Our response in the face of pain and suffering requires a certain emotional intelligence. That connection to your joy story is next.

WINTER

Compassion

Our human compassion binds us the one to the other—not in pity or patronizingly, but as human beings who have learnt how to turn our common suffering into hope for the future.
—Nelson Mandela

As highlighted in the previous chapter, winter is often the most difficult season for enduring common suffering when compared to the challenges of spring, summer, and fall. And the hope, the pathway to heal that suffering sits right in front of us. Pick me! Pick me! Compassion shouts for our attention.

Compassion is an awareness of the suffering of others, and then taking action to relieve that suffering.[61] When you are compassionate, the neuroscience is crystal clear: you are the primary beneficiary. Compassion is the brain's road map that brings you closer to the essence of joy.[62] However, figuring out the best compassionate actions to take, especially for those we love and care about, can be more difficult.

While writing this book, my wife and I were in a yearlong cancer battle with our eleven-year-old golden retriever, aptly named Fibonacci (I am a mathematics teacher at heart, after all). Our girl went four surgeries deep for mast cell tumors that kept returning. Those surgeries were followed by twelve weeks of chemotherapy, steroids, and more.

Fibonacci was a bit beat up by it all; she suffered, she had several scars—ones we could see and ones we could not. Yet her spirit never wavered. She was, first and foremost, loyal to my wife. The two of them spent many months training together when she was a pup. After a year of crate training, Fibonacci eventually managed to make it to our couch and then our bed every night. If you have a pet, you know they have a way of becoming incredibly loving and active members of your family.

To me, it seemed her dignity was dented for sure, but not once did she complain. Not once did she not love us unconditionally. We took a lot of pictures. They show us laughing with her, hugging her, loving her. Whispering to her how brave she was. Sneaking her extra treats. Monitoring her gradual improvement.

Her fourth surgery was an especially difficult and delicate procedure. I picked her up from the vet and carried her to our car. Bandages, stitches, groggy, and more. It was raining as I carried her, and I felt a sense of grief, too hard to explain other than to tell you I got her into the back of my car, moved myself into the driver's seat, and silently shed some tears.

Were we really doing everything in our power to relieve her suffering, or were we making it worse? It was painful to watch a pet we loved so much suffer so much. Worse too, we could not be attuned to her exact needs from our actions, because we could not ask her what she most wanted. Surgeries, chemotherapy, drugs, trips to the doctor once a week—were our perceived acts of compassion what she most needed from us?

No more surgeries. Final answer.

The acts of compassion for Fibonacci, and the questions we were asking regarding what was best to relieve her suffering, were the same questions I often wrestled with for my students when they were suffering. Was I acting with compassion in a way that was best for them?

A fundamental aspect of emotional intelligence is social awareness. *Social awareness* involves being attuned to the emotions and needs of others, fostering positive relationships, and demonstrating empathy and understanding.[63] When you are compassionate, you excel in the social awareness actions required to be a highly effective teacher, leader, counselor, staff, and team member.

Compassionate actions are deeply intertwined with your positive emotional intelligence. *Emotional intelligence* encompasses your ability to recognize, understand, and manage both your own emotions and those of others.[64] At its core, emotional intelligence enables you to navigate emotions effectively. In turn, you become more compassionate and extend your hand to bridge students across the gap between suffering and solace.

It took seven full school year seasons before it occurred to me that maybe we should not assume to know the compassionate acts our students need. Maybe what we believe relieves their suffering isn't what they need at all. Shouldn't we ask our students what they need from us? Students suffering with language difficulties, parental pressures, difficult home lives, hunger, poverty, trauma, bias, or fear need us to be more aware of who they are; they are more than just students. They are members of *our* classroom. *Our* school.

To summarize:

Emotionally intelligent educators develop a

Social awareness of their students and colleagues,

Which in turn informs beneficial

Compassionate acts,

That serve to authentically

Relieve the suffering of those students and colleagues.

MY JOY

And that sequence describes the principal we hired after the interview process (see Winter, Chapter 5: Suffering, page 81). She was the trifecta of the three Cs! In the aftermath of being hired, she delivered.

She modeled a social awareness for effective communication expectations built on kindness, dignity, the assumption of good intentions, and compassionate acts. She facilitated successful conflict resolutions among various stakeholders. She built trust, strengthened relationships, and created a supportive environment where emotional intelligence thrived.

Then, after twenty-three school seasons in that job, she retired. We celebrated her and her impact. And yes, it was emotional. The memory of her impact is fading now. No one can recall the exact programs she installed or changes to improve the facility. What *is* shared are the many ways she validated the work, effort, and results of others. Her social awareness was steady because *she* was steady. Her compassion was modeled

---

What is one way you become more attuned to the suffering of one of your students or colleagues? How do you take action to relieve that suffering?

_____
_____
_____
_____
_____
_____
_____
_____
_____
_____
_____
_____
_____
_____
_____
_____
_____
_____
_____
_____
_____
_____
_____
_____
_____

through her self-compassion. May we all be so blessed to teach and lead and work with such a person.

MY JOY

List three actions you and your colleagues can take to create a more compassionate school and classroom culture to relieve the suffering (big or small) of your students and one another.

___

There is a danger when you approach life with a compassionate heart. That danger is chronic worry, and that connection to joy is next.

WINTER

Worry

I've had a lot of worries in my life, most of which never happened.

—Mark Twain

From a text I sent while writing this book: *I am really worried about how you are going to make it in two weeks with the predicted winter storms coming in. It's not worth it.*

What a word. *Worry*. And in my case, *really worried*. As if just saying "I am worried" is not sufficient. Worry carries the weight of judgment. And, in this case, judgment about a situation in the future that may or may not occur (thanks, Mark Twain!).

I have made it through quite a few winter seasons now. And somehow, winter is the season during the school year when I worry the most. Sometimes too much.

Worried. As in, mentally troubled or concerned, feeling or showing concern or anxiety about what is happening or might happen.[65] Worry occurs over current or future events. Over events or situations that you control and those you do not control.

When you worry, you are often anticipating and mentally preparing for negative events or outcomes in the future—the worst-case scenario, so to speak. The worry is rooted in your *anticipation* of what *might* happen. Worry tends to involve a more prolonged and generalized sense of anxiety about those potential future events. What do you worry about these days? Worry, then, is a cognitive process that involves thinking about potential threats or negative outcomes.

Create a list of everything you are currently worried about at work or at home.

_____
_____
_____
_____
_____
_____
_____
_____
_____
_____
_____
_____
_____
_____
_____
_____
_____
_____
_____
_____
_____
_____
_____
_____
_____

MY JOY

The following "chunks" are from a typical list of daily life I often worry about. Are any of them on your list too?

The health of my students or family members. Financial stability. Family and friendship dynamics. Lesson preparation and delivery. Being a good parent. The educational impact of technology and social media on me and my students. Personal safety and security. Students' daily well-being and performance. Standardized tests. Meeting the needs of relentless parental demands or the absence of any parental influence and control. Time demands for lesson planning, grading, intervention, and teamwork. Balancing school life with personal life.

Staying current in the design and use of new professional knowledge. Knowing how to address student agency and diversity and ensure inclusion. Budget constraints at work, job assignment changes, job exhaustion, and not enough time. That is a lot to worry about!

Worry is closely related to fear. The two often go hand in hand. *Fear* is our basic human emotion triggered by a perceived threat, whether that threat is real or imagined.[66] Fear is also more immediate and usually tied to a specific threat. Both fear and worry are part of the body's natural response to stress and perceived danger and play a role in preparing us to respond to daily challenges and uncertainties.

The downside occurs when our level of worry diminishes our belief in our daily impact. Worry and fear are intertwined in the human experience and often converge in the belief that our actions may be inconsequential, rendering our efforts seemingly futile. The weight of needless worry can morph into a deeper fear, whispering doubts about the significance of our endeavors.

Yes, life is filled with uncertainties. We can and should worry about what tomorrow holds. We should not avoid worry. And yet, we should not let it grip us too tight.

MY JOY

As you review your strategies for avoiding chronic worry, be sure to differentiate between occasional worry, which is a normal part of life and often solvable (in your control), and needless worry, which is usually more generalized (not about a specific, identifiable concern), more pervasive and distressing (interferes with daily work and relationships), and often about elements in life not in your control.

To avoid falling victim to needless worry and to safeguard your joy, you can cultivate mindfulness strategies, such as those in Fall, Chapter 4: Breathe (page 19) or Winter, Chapter 10: Balance (page 103). By practicing mindfulness, you learn to anchor your *awareness* in the present, appreciating the richness of current experiences without being consumed by future worry.

Another helpful mindfulness strategy for worry is to *make time to worry* each week! During your worry appointment, set a timer for fifteen, twenty, or thirty minutes and list your concerns on a piece of paper or in a journal. If you catch yourself worrying about something that doesn't inspire an immediate solution and is outside of your self-appointed time, write it down for your next worry session.

By planning when to worry and for how long, you begin to self-monitor potential hours you may be spending on stressful thinking. The best part of scheduled worry time is that it allows you to compartmentalize to reduce or limit moments of worry the rest of the week.[67] Worry does not need to be the thief of your daily joy.

Our actions, no matter how small, possess the power to shape our own narratives and influence the world around us. While worry and fear may attempt to cast shadows on our endeavors, acknowledging the inherent value of what we do, regardless of the outcome, diminishes worry and becomes an act of resilience toward joy.

It is in this *acknowledgment* that we reclaim agency over our actions, recognizing that, despite future uncertainties, everything we do now matters. Our students are the beneficiaries of our decisions not to give in to chronic worry. Not today, not ever.

Describe how your current worries might be robbing you of joy *today*.

_____
_____
_____
_____
_____
_____
_____
_____
_____
_____
_____

What tips (or life hacks) do you give others for helping them let go of needless worry?

_____
_____
_____
_____
_____
_____
_____
_____
_____
_____
_____

MY JOY

Schedule a twenty-minute worry time in the next few days. List your worries and concerns on the left. Break them into chunks that make sense to you. Are the worries high or low in terms of intensity?

On the right side of the page, write about what you are learning about yourself during your worry time.

Worries and Concerns	What I Am Learning About Myself

In moments of worry, including your planned worry time, it's easy to feel isolated and overwhelmed. However, by embracing the spirit of *gezellig*, you can transform those worry moments into opportunities for the simple joys of shared experiences. *Gezellig* and its connection to worry and joy are next!

WINTER

Gezellig

> *There is nothing like staying at home for real comfort.*
> —Jane Austen

Above all else, *gezellig* **(pronounced** *heh-ZEL-lick*) is a remarkable strategy for developing the resilience and joy needed to overcome the hardship and exhaustion discussed in Winter, Chapter 5: Suffering (page 81) and Winter, Chapter 6: Compassion (page 87).

It was late January of my eighteenth season as an educator when I had two great back-to-back Friday nights, working my way home from the demand of long weeks at school. I love Friday nights and the anticipation of the weekend. It is a gift from our profession.

Those two Friday nights were not the same, but they had the same feeling. They were cozy. Cozy—now there is an interesting word! *Cozy*, as an adjective, means "enjoying or affording warmth and ease."[68]

On that first Friday, I got home around 5:00 p.m., shoveled snow and ice long enough to get my car into the driveway, took a shower, put on my pajamas, got some popcorn (my go-to comfort food) and a warm drink, put on some background music, and settled under a blanket on the couch with a book. It was so cozy that I fell asleep by 8:00 p.m. I woke up on the couch at 6:00 a.m. In case you were wondering, the kids were at sleepovers (*not* at our house)!

Joy.

Share what makes you feel cozy during the winter!

_____
_____
_____
_____
_____
_____
_____
_____
_____
_____
_____
_____
_____
_____
_____
_____
_____
_____
_____
_____
_____
_____
_____

The second Friday was different but had that same warm and cozy feeling. Our good friends down the street came over to the house after dinner (after I cleared the sidewalk and driveway *again*) for some drinks, dessert, and conversation around the table. We talked and played cards until midnight, surprised it was already the next day. Winter was swirling outside, and I was glad we were not the ones walking home!

What most makes you *feel cozy* during the winter months? Is it a bowl of your favorite hot soup, hot tea, or mulled wine under a warm throw blanket? Is it a friendly, intimate atmosphere around you? Is it a quiet evening reading a good book, or hanging out with a small group of family members or friends to talk, laugh, and play games around a table?

MY JOY

There is a Dutch word, already mentioned, that describes this feeling of being cozy.

Gezellig!

It doesn't directly translate into English, but it is a perfect word for those colder days when you are seeking some warmth. *Gezellig* has a broad interpretation beyond just the soup. It is an adjective that can *be* the soup, having the soup with friends, or perhaps the place where you have the soup—such as in front of a fire or in your cozy kitchen.

Gezellig is "a positive, warm emotion or feeling rather than just something physical."[69]

Gezellig encompasses the idea of a welcoming and comfortable atmosphere. This winter, make the decision to pursue the cozy energy and feeling of *gezellig*. Achieving *gezellig* on a Friday night after a long week of work can be a wonderful way to unwind by yourself or connect with your immediate and trusted circle of friends and family. Cultivating *gezellig* on a Friday night can help you feel uplifted, rejuvenated, and balanced after a long winter week of work.

How do you cultivate *gezellig*?

Decide not to stay at work late most days. Prioritize some down time, by yourself or with a small group of others. Instead of the fear of missing out (FOMO), embrace and choose the joy of missing out (JOMO) as a positive alterative sometimes.[70]

Invite your favorite low-drama people over and find a cozy place at home or in a low-key bar or coffee shop. Places that are small, warm, and inviting. Foster meaningful connections on a Friday night to balance out the stress of decision fatigue and more during the week. Engage in conversations, share laughter, and provide mutual support that contribute to the overall feeling of *gezelligheid*. I am certain that is not a word, but it sure sounds good!

Find your inner *gezellig* this winter. There is warmth, comfort, and friendship waiting for you. Be more intimate and fully present with friends and with yourself. Let your home become a place where love resides, memories are created, friends always belong, and laughter never ends.

Ultimately, achieving *gezellig* in the wintertime is about prioritizing your well-being and happiness by clearing space and time for moments when genuine connection and contentment away from your work life can thrive.

On a Friday night, one of our *gezellig* friends asked a familiar question as we sat quietly talking around the table. "What has been the best part of your week?" One at a time, we shared a moment from the past week that felt like a valuable experience of positivity. A moment to be vulnerable as we let others in on our big and small victories along the way.

Gezellig. Try it. Joy is waiting!

MY JOY ♥

Write and share your ideas about how you create intentional moments of *gezellig* in your life, during any season and during any day of the week. Not just in the wintertime or on Fridays! Then share with a trusted friend.

_____
_____
_____
_____
_____
_____
_____
_____
_____

Finding moments of *gezellig* on a Friday or Saturday night after a hectic week at work can serve as a time-out or a pause from the intensity of your work life. It can also serve as a reminder of how important the pause is before responding to your more unpleasant emotions that may occur in the week ahead. Connecting "the pause" to joy is next!

WINTER

Pause

Before you speak, let your words pass through three gates: Is it true? Is it necessary? Is it kind?

—Rumi

"Hit the pause button. I gotta go to the bathroom!"

How convenient it is to have a pause button on our TV remotes. We can cause time to stand still. We can put it on hold until we are ready to hit play again. Too bad we don't have a built-in pause button for our normal, everyday life events.

Taking time to pause before responding to a negative event is a powerful mindfulness tool that allows you to cultivate self-awareness and emotional regulation. In the heat of the moment, it's easy to *react* impulsively, allowing your less-pleasant emotions to dictate your actions. However, by pausing and taking a moment to breathe deeply and center yourself, you create space for reflection and conscious decision making.

The pause serves as a buffer between the event and your response, enabling you to observe your thoughts and feelings without being swept away by them. Through this practice, you gain greater insight into your automatic *reactions*, empowering you to choose more intentional and constructive *responses*.[71]

The act of pausing before reacting, then, provides an opportunity to shift from a *reactive* mindset to a *responsive* one. Rather than being driven by knee-jerk reactions fueled by anger, anxiety, or frustration, you approach the situation with greater clarity, compassion, wisdom, and kindness. Pausing can occur during class or a team meeting, within a family or work conversation, in an email or a text, or in other forms of social media.

What is your go-to "hit the pause button" action when sensing frustration at work or at home?

_____
_____
_____
_____
_____
_____
_____
_____
_____
_____
_____
_____
_____
_____
_____
_____
_____
_____
_____
_____
_____
_____

MY JOY

During my fourteenth season as an educator, I was at work earlier than usual for our winter morning team meetings. A teacher came up to me and said, "Tim, come quick! Call the paramedics; call the nurse! I think Maureen [not her real name] is dying!" I ran down to the room where the team was meeting, and there was Maureen, the team leader, laid out on the floor, blood streaming down her face. I did the best I could to administer first aid until the paramedics got there.

It started with a heated argument about homework between two team members that quickly escalated. One team member finally became so agitated they threw their book at Maureen and hit her in the face, knocking her out of her chair. Twenty-seven stitches later, there were a lot of regrets. All because of the failure to pause.

Event—no pause—unhealthy *reaction*.

Imagine the anguish that lingered for everyone. Now imagine if the book-throwing teammate had just taken a moment to hit pause, walk away, and collect their thoughts and feelings.

Event—pause—healthy *response*.

The *intentional pause* would have allowed the team member to consider alternative perspectives, evaluate the potential consequences of their action (which, in this case, were severe in so many ways), and respond in a way that aligns with desired values and goals (dignity toward everyone).

Regret (see Spring, Chapter 7: Regrets, page 147) is often the residue of temporarily losing connection to kindness (see Spring, Chapter 6: Kindness, page 143).

By integrating mindfulness into our daily lives using the pause, we can cultivate greater emotional resilience, enhance our relationships, and foster a greater sense of inner peace and well-being.[72] There are effective ways to hit the pause button when an event is triggering an unpleasant emotion. What are some routines we can use?

1. *Breathe deeply:* Keep practicing your box-breathing exercises from Fall, Chapter 4: Breathe (page 19) to calm the nervous system and create space between the stimulus and your response. Focus on inhaling deeply through your nose, filling your lungs with air, and exhaling slowly through your mouth.
2. *Practice mindful acknowledgment:* Remember my crazy gas station day from Fall, Chapter 3: Simple Joy (page 15)? Bring your attention to the present by tuning in to your senses. Notice the sounds, sights, and smells around you or the feeling of your feet on the ground. This helps anchor you in the present and reduces the chance for a reactive response.
3. *Count:* Use counting to provide a moment of pause and perspective. This gives you time to collect your thoughts, regulate your emotions, and decide on a more measured and appropriate response of inquiry, as needed.
4. *Engage:* Take a short walk, stretch, or engage in some gentle exercise to release pent-up tension and shift your focus away from the triggering event. Physical movement can help dissipate stress and restore a sense of balance.
5. *Reach out:* Ask for support from a trusted friend, family member, or mental health professional for support and guidance. Sometimes, simply sharing your feelings with someone who listens without judgment can provide immense relief.
6. *Practice self-compassion:* Offer yourself words of kindness and understanding in moments of distress. Remind yourself that it's OK to feel upset or overwhelmed and that you're doing the best you can under the circumstances.

Experiment with these or other pausing strategies to "hit the pause button" and respond to triggering events with greater mindfulness, kindness, and resilience.

Developing your emotional intelligence (discussed in Winter, Chapter 6: Compassion, page 87) isn't about attending a one-time workshop or a weekend retreat to learn strategies for "hitting the pause button" before emotionally responding. That event may be helpful, but the pause is more than an event. It's an ongoing process, forever. A way of life.

Ultimately, how you feel in each moment, and what you *do* with those feelings, determines the quality of your daily life.

MY JOY

Write about your go-to strategies for hitting the pause button when experiencing an event that triggers your more unpleasant emotions. Then share with a trusted friend. And remember to speak with truth and kindness, always!

_____

Writing during daily moments of solitude is one way to process your emotions for a healthy emotional response. That connection between solitude and joy is next!

WINTER

Balance

Solitude is where I place my chaos and awaken my inner peace.
—Nikki Rowe

It's February now. The school year and the winter months are wearing you down.

I can feel my life careening out of balance. The steering wheel of my car is doing some serious vibrating when reaching speeds over twenty-five miles per hour. This is due to my tires. They need to be rotated and balanced, according to my neighbor. He is pretty sure it is from the pothole I keep running over along the highway exiting out of our neighborhood. It's too cold for the work crews to replace the blacktop divots caused by the snow removal equipment, he reminded me.

We are somewhere around six and a half months into the school year (I lost exact track a while ago), and, like my car steering wheel, I am feeling a bit wobbly. My daily high-energy resources are not replenishing as fast as they did back in the fall. If I drive to work in one more snowstorm, I just might lose it.

As I write this winter chapter, it is early in the morning, 4:32 a.m. I am making the time to write before the day's work begins. And I am drinking a cup of coffee out of my favorite mug. It is a misshapen, white cup with one word etched into the ceramic.

Balance.

The mug serves as a daily reminder for my primary route to joy. Stay *balanced* today, it gently reminds me, or in my sleepy fog, sometimes screams at me. Easier said than done. Sometimes,

H̲o̲w̲ would you describe your pursuit for *internal* balance in your daily life?

_____
_____
_____
_____
_____
_____
_____
_____
_____
_____
_____
_____
_____
_____
_____
_____
_____
_____
_____
_____
_____
_____
_____
_____
_____

I notice, I am talking back at my coffee cup message and thinking that cannot be a good sign.

With the madness of another exhausting day of collegial and student relationships, high-energy needs at work and at home, and deadlines awaiting, I also notice small irritations settling in on my brain. I am not my patient, normal self. Maybe it's pothole avoidance syndrome (PAS). I'll give it a name!

With all that I have written about living life with heart, soul, and joy, *balance* is perhaps the most valuable joy gift I can give to myself. I *know* this. Yet it is *so* hard to sustain.

And there is only one path to finding balance in your life. It is not an external pathway like the one described in Fall, Chapter 10: Time (page 43). At best, *external* balance is a temporary fix (necessary but *not* sufficient) to living a more balanced, high-energy, highly relational profession such as ours.

The secret to a well-balanced life is *internal* balance. Daily. And *that* daily decision is found within the walls of seeking solitude.

M̲Y̲ J O Y

Solitude is a critical aspect of a healthy and joyful life. It can boost your mood as you reflect and recharge. When you don't spend much time alone, solitude feels *lonelier*. Those who spend less than 25 percent of their time alone reported high levels of loneliness—as did those who spend 75 percent of their time solo.[73]

Many of us, as educators, are afraid of solitude. But we should not be. Our days are filled with so much noise that the quiet is uncomfortable at first. Yet, incorporating daily solitude into our lives serves as a vital anchor for fostering greater balance in our energy levels and in our relational interactions. By carving out moments of quiet reflection and introspection, you create space to reconnect with yourself and cultivate a deeper sense of self-awareness and *gezellig* (see Winter, Chapter 8: *Gezellig*, page 95).

The intentional routine of daily solitude allows you to recharge and replenish your high-energy emotional reserves. It will also enhance your capacity for empathy, patience, and understanding in your relationships with students, colleagues, and family members.

When you honor your own need for solitude, you become better equipped to engage authentically, hit the pause button as needed, and engage in more meaningful connections by fostering an awareness of others in your interactions.

For all the good and the bad, you are working in a profession and living a daily life at home that needs you to be highly relational every day. Solitude is where you find yourself so you can reach out to others and form real attachments. Ultimately, the door to successful relationships at work and at home is purposeful solitude with an embraced silence.[74]

Solitude empowers you to prioritize your own energy balance while also nurturing supportive and fulfilling connections with others—a primary aspect of our profession. In turn, you become the kind of human being others want on their team.

As you strike a balance between solitude and social relationships, you create a more sustainable and internal balance—one grounded in authenticity, reciprocity, and mutual respect. You just need to *make the time* to make it happen.

Daily solitude might look different to you than it will to your friends. Feel free to customize these ideas to suit your preferences and lifestyle. The following are some routines you can use to get started toward a more *internally* balanced life that embraces daily time in solitude.

- *Make it intentional:* Prioritize moments of quiet reflection in your daily routine. The best periods of solitude come when you plan and look forward to them, instead of just finding yourself alone when plans fall through. Set aside time to read a book, listen to a podcast in a quiet space, or immerse yourself in new ideas and perspectives. Like what I describe in Fall, Chapter 5: Nature (page 23), you can spend time outdoors exploring natural landscapes, parks, or possible snow trails.
- *Make it fun:* Take yourself out to a coffee shop or dinner, take on a new skill, or volunteer. Allow yourself to express your thoughts and emotions through art (without judgment)! Sing and dance to a new playlist. Engage in hobbies or activities you enjoy doing alone, such as gardening, cooking, playing an instrument, yoga, or birdwatching. Allow yourself to connect with the beauty of the natural world and find solace in your surroundings.

- *Make it noise proof:* Eliminate the noise of your daily life. *Screen-free me time* is the most effective way to give your overstimulated brain a break. Disconnect from electronic devices and screens for a designated period each day. Use this time to disconnect from the distractions of technology and reconnect with yourself and the world around you.
- *Make it mindful:* Take a solo walk around your neighborhood, focusing on the sights, sounds, and sensations of the moment. Spend time journaling to reflect on your thoughts, feelings, and experiences. This can help clarify your emotions and gain insights into your teaching world. Practice meditation to cultivate present-moment awareness and inner *gezellig* to anchor your attention and reduce stress.

MY JOY

Use this space to write about your daily routines for seeking solitude.

How do you make solitude intentional?

How do you make solitude fun?

How do you make solitude noise proof?

_____

How do you make solitude mindful?

_____

Who in your family or work life needs to support and help protect your solitude time? Let them know!

_____

Some of you who are reading this book are entering into or existing within your midlife. At this stage of life, balance, passion, purpose, and joy become more elusive. That's next!

WINTER

Midlife

The happiness curve is found in 132 countries. No myth.
—David G. Blanchflower

It's February, and we are emerging from the "midlife" of the current school year. That is good news! Better times lie ahead. Winter blues will soon be left behind! Interestingly, just as each school year has a midlife, you and I also experience midlife years as it applies to our disposition toward happiness, which is different than joy. Happiness is temporal, based on our daily experiences.

The happiness curve refers to a U-shaped pattern that generally depicts how happiness levels tend to change over the course of a person's life. "No ifs, no buts, well-being [happiness] is U-shaped in age."[75]

- *If you are under the age of forty-seven*, your overall happiness with life has been slowly waning.
- *If you are between the ages of forty-seven and fifty-two*, you are in the midlife of, well, life.
- *If you are age fifty-two or older*, celebrate! Your happiness meter trajectory is heading north!

On average, we experience a happiness dip during middle age. The lowest point occurs around ages 47–49, with an average in the United States of 47.2 years old.[76] This period of life, often referenced as a time of midlife crisis, is characterized by feelings of disillusionment, discontent, and a sense of stagnation at work and at home.[77]

By your early fifties and beyond, however, you experience renewed purpose as an educator, greater emotional stability, and a deeper appreciation for life's simple pleasures. The U-shaped happiness curve reveals a rebound. Factors such as increased knowledge for the

What advice for choosing joy would you give someone, despite where they may fall on the happiness curve? How might you help them stay connected to their relationships, joy, and purpose as educators?

_____
_____
_____
_____
_____
_____
_____
_____
_____
_____
_____
_____
_____
_____
_____
_____
_____
_____
_____
_____

job, overall wisdom, stronger social connections, and a greater focus on personal fulfillment contribute to your upward trajectory in happiness.

There has been quite a debate regarding the validity of the happiness curve, and yet more than four hundred international research studies report strong evidence of this U-shaped happiness curve for millions of people.[78] Furthermore, "the happiness curve would not show up in as many data sets and places as it does if it were not to some extent hardwired."[79]

MY JOY

One of my best friends over the years was an outstanding first-grade teacher. Early in her career, Mrs. Williams (not her real name) spent two years teaching in Australia and two years on leave when her son was born. So, she reached her midlife (age forty-eight) during her twentieth year as a teacher.

Like most young teachers, her overall happiness with her work and life was on the rise when she started teaching. But as her school seasons started to stack up, the job was taking its toll on her. Her sense of well-being and satisfaction gradually fell. Summers helped, but she could not quite fully recover the energy needed for the next school season.

I was fourteen years younger, so I did not understand her disillusionment as she reached her late forties. I knew she loved her job, and she was a great first-grade teacher. Yet she was not happy. Her words and actions in her mid forties revealed a constant stream of complaints about her life path. Or so it seemed.

Her son was now off to college and living about five states away. She was questioning the trajectory of her life as a first-grade teacher. Should she have done something else in life? She normally developed and nurtured friendships easily, yet now she seemed to be pushing people away. Those relationships seemed to be a burden. Her love for adventure had leveled off, and her once-strong spirituality seemed dormant too.

My thirty-year-old self could not comprehend her discontent with the difference she was feeling regarding her expectations for life and what she felt her life was becoming. Unbeknownst to me, she was navigating through the waters of a midlife crisis, feeling caught in a tempest of uncertainty about her life's broader purpose. The crisis, in a way, was a blessing for her. It served as a catalyst for introspection, reevaluation, and eventual renewal.

Emerging from the depths of her midlife crisis, she found herself sharing a newfound clarity regarding her purpose—she was, after all, a first-grade teacher! She was loved and beloved. The once-daunting prospect of growing older transformed, for her, into an opportunity for growth, joy, and self-discovery. Her post-midlife journey lasted another fourteen years as a teacher. She finished well. Incredibly great, really.

When she retired, the community celebration included former students and their children. Entire families. The beneficiaries of her chosen life path filled the room! Thankfully, she headed back up the happiness curve embraced by her decision to choose the joy that comes with living authentically and reconnected to her purpose.

Why share Mrs. Williams's story? Because it either has been, could be, or was part of your story.

It is also a micro story within the context of a school season. Our fluctuations in happiness are influenced by various factors, such as workload, stress, relationships, and personal circumstances, all of which are intensified during the difficult winter season. The good news is winter is ending, you are now past the midlife of the school year, and happiness is trending upward as spring awaits!

You have survived the most difficult time of the school year. You have entered and exited the time highlighted as the lowest point in a U-shaped dip regarding your general well-being and happiness in this current school season. You know this intuitively, right? You could sense your happiness slipping away during the endless string of additional winter obstacles.

The purpose of this winter season has been to help you pursue pathways toward chronic joy during the most difficult time of your work year: hang out with colleagues, friends, and family that offer *gezellig*; nurture compassion for those in your work community; and find strength in a balanced life that chooses solitude and silence. Focus not on comparison to and social competition *against* others, but rather move toward social connection and collaboration *with* others.

Therein lies the secret to winter joy. The chapters during this winter season have been designed to flatten the heck out of the happiness curve and reduce the depth of your lowered sense of well-being during winter. Thankfully, that happiness dip is temporary.

MY JOY

Time for a shout-out: Who has brought joy into your world through the midlife of the school season this winter? Describe this person's actions in the space provided, and then be sure to send them a thank-you note!

___
___
___
___
___
___
___
___
___
___
___
___
___
___
___
___
___
___
___
___
___
___

How great it is if you can make it through winter with your emotional and mental wellness reasonably intact. Reflecting *toward* joy is a skill. And that's next.

WINTER

Reflection

No winter lasts forever; no spring skips its turn.

—Hal Borland

There is such delight in winter's end! Yes? Yes!

Winter is ending, and the chill in the air gradually yields to the promise of spring.

The four seasons—autumn (fall), winter, spring, and summer—are caused by Earth's position in relation to the sun. How the Earth is titled toward the sun affects the temperatures and climates in the various regions where each of you live.

The transition into spring marks the changing of seasons. Winter landscapes outside begin to thaw and flowers bloom—everywhere! Regardless of where you live, the end of winter marks a fitting time for reflection. Take a pause to assess progress and then decide how to take full advantage of spring's onset and the longer hours of daylight ahead.

Amid the anticipation of those warmer days, you will find yourself straddling the boundary between endings and beginnings. The *school year* is approaching its conclusion (three months away), yet the spring *season* is just beginning. Thus, the March entrance into spring alerts you to take a time-out and reflect on your winter journey as it ends.

You ask and answer reflective questions about the results of your winter life. What lessons did you learn about your physical, mental, and emotional wellness and successes thus far? What challenges have you faced and overcome? What have been your best and worst experiences during these past three months? The ending of winter's retreat now offers a prime opportunity to take stock of your successes and setbacks, the triumphs and tribulations that have shaped you as a teacher and leader during *this* academic year.

As you prepare to transition from one season to the next, consider how to carry forward these insights gleaned from your reflections. What adjustments need to be made *now* as you embark on the final leg of the school year? What goals and routines need to be sustained and pursued? What strategies can be employed to achieve them? How can your experiences during winter inform your approach toward students and colleagues during the spring months ahead?

As daylight increases and brings sunshine to your face, find joy in the whirlwind of activity that accompanies the end of the school year. Enjoy the renewed energy that comes with the hustle and bustle of spring. A relief and a celebration.

Take a deep breath and use your reflections to help focus your time and effort on finishing well as you climb the final steep steps ahead. Allow your reflection on the past six months to inform your disposition for the next three months of work; use the prompts that follow, as needed. What would you like to tell your future self when winter hits once again next school season?

MY JOY

What would you like to tell your future self when the next winter season arrives?

Winter reflections:
Reflect on personal experiences, challenges, and accomplishments during this winter season. Consider any lessons learned and how they inform future actions and endeavors.

_____
_____
_____
_____
_____
_____
_____
_____
_____
_____
_____
_____

Winter experiences:

Reflect on memorable winter adventures and outings. Share any positive experiences from your favorite indoor or outdoor activities, the holidays, or your favorite moments of *gezellig*.

_____
_____
_____
_____
_____
_____
_____
_____
_____
_____
_____
_____
_____
_____
_____
_____

Planning for next winter:

Start thinking ahead to the next winter season. Consider activities, trips, or goals to look forward to, as well as any adjustments or preparations to make for a more fulfilling winter experience *next* school season.

_____
_____
_____
_____
_____
_____
_____
_____
_____
_____
_____
_____
_____
_____
_____
_____

Winter wellness:

Explore strategies for maintaining physical, mental, and emotional wellness during the winter months. Discuss self-care practices, relaxation techniques, and ways to boost your mood and energy.

___

Winter gratitude:

Express gratitude for the beauty, lessons, and experiences of the winter season. Reflect on winter's unique qualities and the ways it enriches life with its challenges and charms.

___

Winter transitions:

Explore ways to transition from winter to spring in daily routines, activities, and mindsets. Discuss plans for outdoor activities, spring cleaning, or embracing the change to a new season and holidays.

___

Winter has been a season of showing up for joy despite the hardships that come with the season and its timing during the middle of the school year. The art of showing up and its connection to joy are next!

WINTER

*I will embrace the moment.
Forget my past mistakes,
And remember that just showing up
Is sometimes all it takes.*

—Amy Grant

Dear reader: I am writing this final chapter in part 2 different from the others. It is written as a dialogue between me and you as we approach the end of winter. I hope winter has been a season of joy, courage, *gezellig*, and strength for you. Your voice is in italics. Enjoy!

Show

Winter. Ugh.

Right, ugh. A long three months.

Showing up most days?

Most of them. Winter wore me down. Grind, grind, grinding away.

Despite the hardship of the winter school season, describe a moment when you realized that *showing up* and staying engaged was all it took to be the educator you were meant to be.

You're tired?

Yes, tired. Of the cold. The winds and rains. The snow. The relentless gray skies. The short daylight. The additional outerwear. The heavy lifting.

Winter messes with your mood?

Sometimes—I'm seeking silence.

Winter seeps into your suffering?

Deeply. I'm seeking less self-judgment.

Winter cheers on your thoughts of quiet quitting?

No! I'm hanging on to my meaning and purpose.

Winter shouts and shuts you out.

Yes, I'm taking brisk walks outdoors.

Winter can complicate daily life.

Simplify! Simplify! That's what I did!

Winter builds into the art of showing up, right?

Yes! I was steadfast, persistent, unwavering, determined, resilient, and intentional.

You learned to use winter, not the other way around.

Winter is ending. Thank goodness.

Winter yields to spring.

How thoughtful!

Funny, winter acts as if it doesn't really know you. It isn't leaving because you said, "Get out!"

Something to do with the tilt of the Earth's axis and its orbit around the sun, yes?

Yes. Ugh. That means another winter season next year.

Winter will start and end again.

And you will show up, once again. You always do.

"I will embrace the moment. Forget my past mistakes, and remember that just showing up is sometimes all it takes"?[80]

Exactly.

MY JOY

Winter:
A Season to Be Resolute
Your Conclusions

During this winter season, which of the joy actions in Winter chapters 1–13 most resonated with your current personal and professional joy journey—a school season of heavy lifting? In reflection, what are three to five brief takeaways about growing strong during the winter season?

— **MY** J O Y ♥ —

Write about your favorite takeaways from this winter season that might serve your overall joy journey as an educator and your well-being as you transition into finishing well during the spring season, heading down the stretch toward the school year's end.

_____
_____
_____
_____
_____
_____
_____
_____
_____

You can check out my video here, where I provide my conclusions and insight from Part 2: Winter—A Season to Be Resolute. Thanks for joining the winter journey with me. It was hard!

PART 3

SPRING: A SEASON TO SHOW RESOLVE

Growing Strong in a Season of Finishing Well

Freedom! It's the first day of spring. The winter months of the school season are now in the rearview mirror. You are moving ever forward. March, April, and May! They are a breath of fresh air as a subtle internal disquiet of accountability awaits. The work suddenly becomes more urgent. Only three months left to get students ready for *next year*. State tests are just around the corner, rearing their ugly heads.

Spring presents a season of finishing what you started almost seven months ago. *Finishing well* is a joy challenge. The end is in sight. Can you make it to the finish line?

During March (Spring, chapters 1–4), you finish well by leaving behind winter's heavy lifting and emerge with new resolve to focus on your joy journey by acknowledging the joy of others, sustaining your credibility, and *preparing* your students and colleagues for the rigors of the assessments and performance expectations in April and May.

In April, you finish well by making final recommendations or sharing information for students moving to the next grade level, a new school building, or beyond graduation. You set your sights on the challenges of ending one school season while simultaneously planning for the next. You become more aware of your relationship success during this current school year and seek feedback from others. Were you wise, credible, generous, and kind (Spring, chapters 6–8)? Do you have regrets of action or inaction, and above all else, did you overcome any regrets by making the impossible seem possible?

May is a time for adding another finishing-well ending in a tapestry of collected school seasons. Deep relationships and deeper connections that mark another school year are almost all in the books. Graduations, promotions, and end-of-year celebrations bring a sense of *meraki, commouvere,* and *ubuntu* (Spring, chapters 9–12) stories. There is closure to your hard work and a reminder of those benefiting from your year of sustained effort. Those warm connections are a core feature of optimal and, sometimes, melancholy human experiences.

You take pictures, knowing the memories will eventually fade away. The people in the pictures will most likely shift and change during the next school year. You feel a bit raw from the labor of the past nine months as you wrap up the academic year and look forward to a well-deserved season of rest during the summer. However, in this spring season of closure, community, and abundance, joy finds its delight in you, your effort, your wisdom, your actions, and who you were and are in each moment of the school year. And you know, once again, your work finds its worth.

SPRING

Finishing

Finishing well is more important than starting well, for it is not the beginning that earns praise, but the ending.

—Anonymous

Spring is in the air. March is here. Can you see it? Smell it? Joy!

Finally, winter is over. The heavy lifting of the school season is melting away.

Springtime breaks us out of our winter dormancy and into a time of the year with new beginnings. Flowers are blossoming, birds are singing, trees are leafing out—nature wakes up and says hello. Let's go!

Farming communities are planting new crops, and people are starting gardens. The springtime of nature symbolizes a fresh start and the beginning of a new cycle of growth and vitality. The warmer weather and increased daylight hours create a sense of optimism and energy.

MY JOY

Overall, the combination of natural, cultural, and psychological factors makes springtime a symbolic and tangible representation of new beginnings, making it

Write a list of your favorite springtime outdoor beginnings each year.

_____
_____
_____
_____
_____
_____
_____
_____
_____
_____
_____
_____
_____
_____
_____

a season filled with promise, potential, and possibility following the recent winter season.

Ironic though, isn't it?

The spring season is the reverse paradox of fall. In the calendar year, spring signals new growth and beginnings. Yet, in our professional school year calendar, spring signals an *ending*. We are headed into the final turn. And the question we need to answer, as the ending awaits on the horizon (we can *almost* see it), is this:

Will we finish well?

Can we use the renewed energy of the springtime that surrounds us to take a deep and collective breath and then plow into the hard work remaining before the summer season pulls us and our students away? We have just a few months left to make a difference. Springtime of the school year is about completing the mission. To finish what we started six months ago.

∞

Peter (not his real name) was not finishing well. No joy. None. At least none he was showing to his students and colleagues. We sat in my office in silence. I had just finished his three-day observation and evaluation. The results were not good.

He had almost no credibility left with his peers and his students, and the steady drumbeat of his constant complaints was wearing everyone thin. It was early March, and I was his immediate supervisor as the director of mathematics and science. He was my colleague and my friend. And yet, his colleagues were watching closely to see how I would respond to his choice to be miserable, his overall lack of professionalism, and their concerns that his students would not be prepared for the end-of-school-year expectations, much less coursework expectations for the following year.

He was not finishing well. He had not been finishing well for a few years now. These were the thoughts running through my mind as we sat in silence.

The silence lasted about five minutes and felt like a lifetime. Finally, I asked him a finishing-well question: "Can you remember a time in your professional career when you were able to acknowledge the joy of your students and colleagues?" He said he did not know what I meant.

I asked him if he wanted to recapture his credibility with others and cheer on their joy. He said he didn't care about it. No one else cares, anyway. More silence.

It was getting late in the day on a Friday afternoon. I decided to give Peter an assignment for Monday morning. We would cover his morning teaching duties so he could meet me at a local pancake house for breakfast. At that meeting, he was to describe what he thought it meant to finish the school year well and bring a list of five actions he would take between now (early March) and the end of the year to finish well.

I indicated I would bring my list for him, too, and we would compare and decide on the next steps. I reminded him he was a professional. As such, he had an obligation to his students to finish well. I also told him he was important to me and, therefore, I would not give up on him.

As we departed for the weekend, I reminded him of a simple truth—once we acknowledge we are professionals, *we no longer get to do whatever we feel like doing*. We are expected to be prepared every day, be radically kind, and provide hope for the learning and improvement of others.

As part of my research for this book, I asked teachers, counselors, principals, and support staff members how they finish well during the spring of each school year. What does it mean? What does it look like? Does it bring them joy to finish well?

Their overall responses, their reasons *why* it is important to finish well, are summarized as follows: When you finish well, you leave a lasting impact on your students and colleagues. And when you don't, no one benefits. Especially you. Knowing you are credible, prepared every day, connected, kind, and gave your best effort through the end of the school year is what brings joy.

More specifically, the responses I received fell into three advice categories for personal and professional benefits to *finishing well* each spring season.

1. *Acknowledging joy:* When you acknowledge the joy of others, your personal satisfaction and sense of accomplishment are part of your self-efficacy growth that leads to finishing well. When *you* finish well, your students and colleagues maximize *their* effort, achieve *their* goals, and increase *their* learning and *their* self-efficacy. Bringing them joy and improving their

self-esteem will enhance your joy.[81] Finishing well is hard. The joy rewards are great (see Spring, Chapter 2: Acknowledging Joy, page 127).

2. *Building credibility:* Consistently finishing well builds credibility and trust in your professional abilities. Students will want to be in your class! Colleagues will want to hang out with you! When you consistently deliver high-quality results and meet or exceed expectations for student learning, you earn the *belief* (a key word in the credibility game) and the confidence of others as they choose to follow your lead (see Spring, Chapter 3: Credibility, page 131).

3. *Preparing for future success:* Finishing well sets the stage for future student success. You also establish a track record for having a pathway to excellence as you become more reliable. More professional. By consistently demonstrating your ability to inspire students and improve student learning, you position yourself with increased confidence and self-efficacy to take on new opportunities and challenges in future school years—an aspect of your work life that brings daily joy (see Spring, Chapter 4: Preparation, page 135).

By prioritizing finishing well during the spring season, you maximize your impact, build credibility, and set yourself up for continued success and fulfillment at work.

MY JOY

As spring begins, look ahead toward the end of the school year. What does it mean to finish well over the next three months? How will you sustain your joy as the school year ends?

_____
_____
_____
_____
_____
_____
_____
_____
_____
_____
_____
_____
_____

The spring chapters that follow are designed to help you finish well during March, April, and May. You create joy when you finish strong. Let's begin!

SPRING

Acknowledging Joy

Spend less time being interesting, and more time being interested.
—John Gardner

You have done the heavy lifting of winter. How did you emerge from it? You are standing in March now—are you closer to full exhaustion or to full engagement with the energy required to finish the next three months well? Maybe you are somewhere in between. Your mental and emotional health did not emerge unscathed, right?

MY JOY

∞

I did not spend much time considering emotional health when I was in my early seasons of teaching. By season ten, however, the full school year was taking its toll on me. I had moved three times and was in my third teaching job by then. My wife and I had two young children (one and three years old), and I was once again back in graduate school to become certified as a potential administrator.

Like many of you reading this book, we were working extra side jobs to pay bills. I had been coaching a winter

On average, most days, how do you feel? Briefly explain.

_____
_____
_____
_____
_____

On average, most days, how do you make the people around you feel? Briefly explain.

_____
_____
_____
_____
_____
_____
_____

sport that just ended and was teaching at the local community college on Saturdays. Springtime would steamroll in, and I barely had a chance to notice the joy of others, much less my own emotional health, wellness, and joy. In short, March would arrive, and I was reasonably overwhelmed on the inside. It occasionally showed on the outside.

Most importantly, though, the high-speed energy of the start to my season the previous fall was notably absent. Students were not getting the best version of me during the springtime months. My levels of preparation, feedback, and attention to their needs were not the same. The way I made my colleagues and students feel was not a feeling of joy. I knew it, felt it, and did not know what to do about it. My feeling about hanging on in the springtime of the school year was this: *Just get to Memorial Day!*

Yet, there was always one saving grace for me, invariably, somewhere during the springtime journey. *The joy of my students* and my most-trusted colleagues would bring me joy!

This spring, how much time will you spend trying to model and engender joy despite the challenges you face each day? Practice giving focused attention to others this spring. Practice deep listening by smiling, making eye contact, and not interrupting, and minimize making judgments about what others are saying. What is the joy role model for communication you will demonstrate this spring? There is a greater good you can contribute to your students, colleagues, and families when *you* are fully present and recognize their joy, even when they can't see it. Joy *acknowledgment* is a *choice*.

As my colleague Tina Boogren and I write in our educator wellness materials, our mental and emotional health and the quality of our relationships, at work and at home, are intimately interconnected.[82] During March, the less time we spend improving our own mental and emotional suffering, the more unaware we are of how our emotional state negatively impacts others.

Conversely, if we worked hard during the winter season to keep our emotional wellness in order, then we are on the road to acknowledging the joy of others during the spring season. We can help create joy for others by developing confidence and competence for the difficult tasks (like state testing) that lie ahead.

It is never too late to overcome the lingering fog from the heavy lifting of the winter months. Acknowledging joy—acknowledging and connecting to the joy of others—just may be the best emotional-wellness strategy and action yet!

The early springtime struggle to finish well is solved by looking outward. Although it is our job to support our students and colleagues, it is essentially a way to help ourselves, too. It will make us feel good. Studies show experiencing and acknowledging the joy of others makes us more compassionate and satisfied with life.[83]

Joy is found in our connection with others. In our *ubuntu* (see Spring, Chapter 12: *Ubuntu*, page 167). It's a subconscious, almost visceral feeling that stems from the brain's limbic system, believed to control our emotions. Unlike happiness, joy involves little cognitive awareness—you just feel good without thinking about it—but it's more enduring.[84]

To deepen your ability to acknowledge the joy of others, use the steps provided in the MY Joy section.

Repeating this practice will connect your joy to the joy of others and bring you more joy. That would be a good life cycle to travel!

MY JOY

Joy does not need to be complex. It is a choice. Make the choice to use the *acknowledging joy* steps as a road map for your "joy of others" plan!

Step 1: Find a comfortable place to begin and bring a notebook.

Step 2: Visualize a person or situation at work that brings you a sense of joy. It might be a students' writing, humor, victory, progress, or performance. Or it could be the success of a colleague who completed a difficult task, or a significant change that led to improved student learning. Write about that person (or persons) and their joy actions in the space provided.

_____
_____
_____
_____
_____

Step 3: Connect emotionally to this person's joy. Write about what you are feeling.

_____
_____
_____
_____
_____

Step 4: Write a short note or email and thank them, appreciate their joy and effort, and wish them well. Tell them how their joy brings you joy. Yes, *tell them*! *You can write a draft of the note in the space provided.*

Step 5: As appropriate, expand your focus to a team of colleagues at work and appreciate their effort and success. Then repeat step 4. Which team or teams might that be?

Acknowledging joy is a great springtime strategy. It also allows students and colleagues to see you as a credible resource and source. Which, in turn, allows others to believe in and follow you as they also grow strong to the finish line!

SPRING

Credibility

Without character, there is no credibility; and without credibility, there is no trust.

—Warren Bennis

It's still March. Less than three months to go now. You are tired. Your energy is dissipating. Right about now you are closing in on a well-deserved spring break. A short rest stop before you cross the finish line. Guess what?

Spring break is a great time for a credibility check!

It's time to check in on how your daily actions are increasing or decreasing the belief others have in you as their teacher and leader. Is your credibility still intact after the long winter-season slog? This is a hard question, as your credibility is based on what others (students, parents, and colleagues) *believe* about you. And their beliefs are determined by *your* actions.

Ugh.

Your intentionality toward sustaining credibility with others for the next three months is one aspect of finishing the school year well. There is a lot of teaching and learning time left, a lot of convincing your students and colleagues to keep trying, to keep learning. Credibility can slowly drip away. Then, your impact diminishes.

What is *credibility* anyway?

Turns out credibility is your ability to sustain the "quality or power of inspiring belief. [You are] good enough to be *effective*."[85] Think of all the stakeholders (students, colleagues, parents, and more) you impact and influence. How well do you inspire their belief in you and your ability to excel in your role with the school or district?

Survey three trusted students or colleagues. Ask them to provide you with some brief reasons why they believe you are a credible person and how you might improve. Seek honest feedback! In this space, note some highlights of what you heard.

_____
_____
_____
_____
_____
_____
_____
_____
_____
_____
_____
_____
_____
_____
_____
_____
_____
_____
_____
_____
_____

Do those stakeholders view you as a credible teacher, counselor, school staff member, or school site or central office leader? If you surveyed your closest friends, would they indicate you are a credible person? I hope so! Collect some data and find out.

MY JOY

Knowing you are making progress in your work life will keep you connected to your daily joy when you are exhausted and tired.[86] If you can stay connected to your greater purpose (helping all students to the finish line), it will diminish the cynical feelings and negativity that occasionally creep in. As you develop your self-efficacy (your confidence and competence to help every student learn), students' and colleagues' brains apply mental shortcuts to judge your daily credibility quickly and efficiently.[87]

How do you improve your credibility with students and colleagues? There are three actions you can take during the rest of March, April, and May that will help impact the belief others have in you.[88]

1. *Be competent:* Students and colleagues thrive on clarity. Likewise, they are repelled by confusion. Teaching and leading others must be concise, develop active student meaning-making, and be relevant to those you teach (students or colleagues). Model a continuous and deep understanding of the standards you teach and stay up to date with current research trends in education. Incorporate relevant content and engaging activities into your lessons that demonstrate your expertise. You are aware of the effort given by students and colleagues to listen to you. Are you interesting? Are your words engaging? Do you reach a diminishing return during direct instruction, limiting others' ability to stay focused and interested? Do you stop talking long enough to listen? Do you break down concepts and skills into manageable chunks using language students and colleagues understand?

2. *Be passionate:* Yes, you may be tired. Who isn't? Exude enthusiasm anyway! The origin of enthusiasm is Greek—*enthous* (inspired by) and *theos* (meaning *God* or *spirit*).[89] Do students and colleagues sense you are inspired by your use of high positive energy, kind facial expressions, positive vocal intonation and affirmation, and a daily dedication that models how to finish strong by signaling how much you care about your and their commitment to the work ahead? Enthusiasm is contagious because it's enjoyable and attractive. By communicating information clearly, concisely, positively, and effectively—and by using a variety of instructional strategies and techniques to engage students and facilitate understanding—you model how to rock it out to the end!

3. *Build trusting relationships:* Students and colleagues need to know you care about them personally and care about how they learn. Do your students and colleagues confidently ask you for help? Do you manage your energy and anxiety so you can remain calm and confident around others? Is your *gezellig* (see Winter, Chapter 8: *Gezellig*, page 95) evident at work? Are you fully present with students and colleagues? Are you compassionate yet humble? Do you respect boundaries? Do you provide feedback based on facts and not unpleasant emotions? Are you willing to grow and be flexible? Do you *make the time* (see Fall, Chapter 10: Time, page 43) to get to know students and colleagues individually and show genuine interest in their lives?

By my fourteenth season of teaching, I had become the director of mathematics and science at my school. One of my teachers, Claudia (not her real name), came into my office and said, "You are a smart guy, so you need to figure this out. You are losing all credibility as a teacher and leader. I drew the short straw, so I was chosen to come in here and tell you this." I was a bit stunned by her directness and dismayed that despite how hard I was working to establish credibility, I was failing.

When I pressed her on how this was happening, it became clear it was not my competence or passion. It was my failure to build a culture of trust. When pressed further, Claudia revealed that I failed to keep my word and meet deadlines; *everyone* felt this way. She told me quite bluntly that my use of the phrase "I will try to get it done" had grown tiresome. She said it let me off the hook and that my word was no good anymore. Her message to me was clear: *We don't trust your word, and "trying" is not cutting it.* The clarity of her verbal slap in the face was exactly the wake-up call I needed.

From that moment on, I stopped using the *inaction* phrase, "I'll try to do . . . ," and instead, used the *action* phrase, "I will do." Action does, indeed, speak so much louder than words.

MY JOY

Which of the following credibility actions would help you this spring as you earn and re-earn others' belief in you before it is too late? Why did you choose this action?

Be competent:
How do you continuously deepen your understanding of academic knowledge and stay up to date with current research and best practices?

_____
_____
_____
_____

Be passionate:
How do you work to develop your relationship skills and model enthusiasm with positive emotional communication?

_____
_____
_____
_____

Be trustworthy:
How do you create a culture of positive caring and connections? How well do you honor your promises to others?

_____
_____
_____
_____

As March ends, a fierce urgency creeps in. The time for test preparation is *now*. Next!

SPRING

Preparation

Train before it comes.
—Seneca

Can you hear it? The assessment train is coming. The days of accountability are just a few weeks away now. Are you prepared for it? *Now* is the time for last-minute repairs to standards not yet learned. Finishing this school year well depends on demonstrating your collective competence with colleagues as you develop the strength in students' assessment performances.

MY JOY

Chances are your MY Joy response in the margin will be filled with more expletives than joyful thoughts. However, fear not! Preparation makes you, your students, and your colleagues braver.

You and I chose a *social-sector* profession. The outcome of our school season of work is *not* profits and more money. Our outcome—our time and effort to train and practice, our greatness—is shoehorned into a very singular focus: the *performing* character and the *moral* character development of our students by the end of the school season.

Assessment training and preparation are essential to finishing the school year well. How does the phrase *assessment training and preparation* make you feel?

_____
_____
_____
_____
_____
_____
_____
_____
_____
_____
_____

And now we are nearing the end.

Performing indicates *every* student meets the proficiency expectations of our grade-level or course-based essential standards during April and May testing. It is a daunting greatness we pursue. *Moral* (becoming good) indicates *every* student develops improved character that eventually leads to becoming a responsible citizen. While difficult to measure, that's the goal, nonetheless.

We chose a profession that expects us to connect mentally and emotionally to the *outcomes* of our work life. In other words, to the measured *performance* of our students.

We chose a profession that, like it or not, is *publicly* measured by student performance on state or national assessments in the spring of every school year.

This is, after all, partly what we have been training our students for, correct? And there is nothing to fear if we collaborated with colleagues to teach and practice with great competence and confidence.

And now, we are near the end of March. State testing stares at us in the mirror. The teaching of new standards recedes, replaced by the tide of practicing standards that need student correction, feedback, and action. We act with the urgency of *now*. Before it is too late.

Testing may seem like the enemy, but experience and continued training over the next few weeks can mitigate the perceived danger. Repetition leads to preparation, preparation leads to confidence, and confidence leads to courage.

We can do this!

Focused practice is the most important action right now. With practice, you take students and colleagues on a journey of actions and muscle memory in their minds. What are they to do when encountering various situations during the big test? You ask purposely tough questions, more complex than the ones they need to prepare for, and you help them get comfortable with the discomfort. And you do it a thousand times while there is no pressure. Knowing what to do and how to do it is a big help. But preparation is the secret sauce of the brave on game day.

By March, student motivation and engagement can drag. Every year, one of my colleagues, Linda (not her real name), and I prepared our students for the upcoming state assessments by making it fun, engaging, repetitive, and rigorous.

In our case, spring break was always the third week of March. Our plan was to engage our students in a unique form of review right after they returned from break. We would do the following.

1. Group students into teams of five or six around specific standards for which many of them needed additional time for practice and review.

2. Ask student teams to perform ten-minute mini presentations in the tone, style, word usage, and mannerisms of their teacher (either me or Linda), and create a review packet (digital or otherwise) for the class.

3. Linda's students would present their understanding of the assigned mathematics standard(s) to the class in front of me. My students would do their presentations in my classroom, but in front of Linda. We then rated each presentation based on how closely it mimicked their teacher's presentation style. We had fun while trying to intensely review with our students.

After one week of this type of review, we then dug deep into student practice packets (based on our assessment feedback throughout the year) filled with the tasks for the standards needing additional practice before the big April event. We wanted to reinforce the idea that learning is a continuous journey of growth, practice, and rediscovery rather than just state assessment outcomes. Preparation is what brave and courageous people do in life. This was our message. We didn't demand they prepare. We showed them how and then *expected* them to act and train *together*.

Connecting test preparation to springtime review and renewal may seem like a strange joy connection to you. Yet, the joy part is not about the state or local tests per se. As this chapter title suggests, it is more about the loop of corrective feedback and student action. The journey to the test.[90] It is our responsibility to provide an iterative learning structure that moves students ever forward as they transition beyond us with the preparations necessary for the next school year.

Is success in the previous year not our hope for the students *we will inherit* as we start a new school year just a mere five months from now? May those teachers, counselors, specialists, and administrators be thinking of you, as they help their students finish well this spring school season and get them ready for the next school year ahead!

MY JOY

A *proactive mindset* leads to a greater sense of control, confidence, efficacy, and peace of mind, contributing to your overall well-being and happiness.[91] How are you modeling a positive and proactive mindset about springtime state testing?

An *accomplishment mindset* can bring joy and fulfillment to daily life.[92] How are you creating a sense of confidence and accomplishment by successfully preparing students for the standards they have identified as not yet learned—before it is too late?

Overall, practice and preparation before it's too late can contribute to greater well-being, confidence, and joy in daily life. The hard work of preparation leads to a story of engagement and connection to your work life. Those joy connections are next!

SPRING

Engagement

When some of us are on the edge, we are all on the edge.
—Lady Gaga

Take a moment to answer a quick question in the MY Joy space.

MY JOY

If you answered any part of the MY Joy prompt with a *no*, you are not alone. As of this writing, only 31 percent of the global workforce in the United States and Canada would say yes to being fully engaged in their daily work life (all three seasons of fall, winter, and spring). Additionally, 17 percent would say no to being fully engaged during all three seasons, and 52 percent would say yes to being fully engaged sometimes during the three seasons.[93]

And now it's April. Despite the brightness and energy of a sunny spring blooming outside, you just might be running on fumes right about now. Staying fully engaged in your work life is necessary *and* challenging. Anger, stress, worry, and sadness are often on the rise. And it takes everything you have in your inner core to fight it off and choose joy.

"**Do** you have the greatest job in the world?" Answer *yes*, *no*, or *sometimes*. Answer based on the three seasons you've experienced so far this school year: fall, winter, and spring. Provide a brief description.

_____
_____
_____
_____
_____
_____
_____
_____
_____
_____
_____

We are asked and tasked to relentlessly be reliable and stable while acknowledging our daily need to stay balanced as a full-time, intentional pursuit. Finishing well these last two months, near the end of a long school year, happens when we stay fully connected to and engaged in our work.

And it matters, right? Our students and colleagues depend on us to optimize our daily work life down the stretch. The worst trait we could display right now is to become actively disengaged in our work life as we race to the finish. Everyone around us would suffer. What shall we do then to stay connected and engaged in the joy of our daily work?

You might wonder what happened to Peter when we met on the Monday after our Friday meeting in March (refer to Spring, Chapter 1: Finishing, page 123, before you read on). Remember, he was extremely disengaged from his daily work life.

We met at the pancake house and sat outside. It was an unusually bright and sunny spring day in stark contrast to the stormy conversation ahead. His teaching life had fallen into that bracket of 17 percent of the workforce that is completely disengaged from their jobs. I had given a lot of thought to our conversation from the previous Friday and decided to take a different approach.

I started by asking him a big-picture question: "If you had a choice, what work other than teaching would have given you deeper satisfaction and joy?" I was searching for what connected and mattered to his heart and mind.

I then asked him a series of engagement questions. I asked him to identify his best skills, followed by what he remembers he enjoyed most about being an educator. I asked him what most annoyed him about his work *this* school year. How could he do more of what he most enjoyed and less of what annoys him? If he had the power to teach any grade level or course and decide his own schedule the following school year, what would it be?

I then asked him to take stock of his current teaching situation. To be honest with me. His situation wasn't hopeless, I said, but I needed to know what part of his work routine he hated. My only caveat was that he did not act like a victim and blame other people. I wanted a sincere response that reflected his conviction that "I want to have a better teaching life."

I was kind yet honest with him and told him he was difficult to be around, often making life miserable for those around him—both students and colleagues. Worse, he was not helping his younger colleagues because he was so worn down by his own suffering. I knew he would hate to hear this, yet I knew learning for *his* students was also on the line.

I told him as gently as I could, and with grace toward him as a person, that he needed to stop waiting for *other people* to make him feel better about his job and his life as an educator. Self-compassion required. Only *he* could act to relieve his suffering. I told him I would clarify the direction and actions he needed to take, but ultimately, he had to choose his finishing-well path.

"*You* own *you*," I said.

Breakfast came, and we sat silently for quite a while. It was uncomfortable, but I felt the need to let him process our discussion. Only then did we compare our lists and start a plan for the next few months and the summer season. We outlined the small steps he could take now to squeeze more joy and meaning out of his work life in the future. When we finished eating, I gave him one last bit of tough love.

I told him that if his choice was to stay miserable for a sustained period ahead, then he should quit. And if he can't quit, then I would assign him to do something else. His current state of engagement was not doing himself, our school, our students, or our parents any favors by loathing his job each day.

Strangely, I then told him I loved him. No matter what he decided.

Overall, while being fully engaged in your work life may not guarantee joy, it can create conditions that support and enhance joyful experiences in life. As described in the fall and winter seasons, you increase your capacity for experiencing joy and fulfillment at work by cultivating conditions of emotional regulation, gratitude, perspective, authenticity, and meaningful relationships.[94]

Be confident. Stay engaged. Finishing well is so worth it when this spring season is over. Your students and colleagues need access to the best engagement version of you that exists!

MY JOY

Answer the following workplace engagement questions.

Identify your best skills.

_____
_____
_____
_____
_____

What do you most enjoy about being an educator?

_____
_____
_____
_____
_____

What annoys you most about your work? How do you minimize that annoyance?

_____
_____
_____
_____
_____

How could you ask to do more of what you most enjoy and less of what annoys you? Who do you need to ask? How do you need to prepare for the conversation?

_____
_____
_____
_____
_____

Kindness and joy are intimately related. It is never too late to develop kindness toward others, including those you think do not deserve it. That is next!

SPRING

Kindness

What I regret most in my life are failures of kindness.
—George Saunders

There is something about spring that brings kindness to my heart. I am not sure why exactly, other than I can get outside more easily, I feel lighter, and—now that we are into April—I more deeply sense the stress my students and colleagues are under. There is the pressure of preparing for and taking state assessments and the additional stress of wrapping up transitions for *this* school year while beginning the planning and preparations for the *next* school season that is four-plus months away.

Double-whammy time.

Kindness required. There are no takebacks. You can't exactly go back in time and wish you had been kinder these past ten months. You can only surge forward to the end *before* it is too late.

Studies indicate that merely witnessing acts of kindness can have positive side effects on you, such as increased self-esteem, increased empathy and compassion, and improved mood. Kindness increases your sense of connectivity with others and enhances your relationships in general.[95] Random, yet intentional, acts of kindness are associated with a reduction in your social anxiety symptoms.[96]

When you are either thinking about kind acts, witnessing kind acts, or engaging in kind acts toward your students or colleagues, biochemical changes happen in your brain. Physiologically, being kind boosts serotonin and dopamine. Joy! These neurotransmitters in your brain provide feelings of satisfaction and well-being and cause the pleasure-reward centers in your brain to light up. More joy! Endorphins, which are your body's natural pain killer, can also be released.[97]

Start your day with this question: "How am I going to practice kindness today?"

Document your evidence of kindness to others and to yourself during this spring day.

_____
_____
_____
_____
_____
_____
_____
_____
_____
_____
_____
_____
_____
_____
_____
_____
_____
_____
_____
_____
_____
_____
_____

Moreover, kindness has been shown to improve mood and decrease blood pressure and cortisol—a hormone directly correlated with stress levels.[98] Kindness, then, can increase your sense of connectivity with others and help improve your relationships at work and at home. Kindness *is* contagious.

Sign me up for some kindness!

MY JOY

It wasn't until I started doing the research for this chapter that I realized, intentionally or unintentionally, I surround my work life with colleagues who are kind in spirit and in action. And their actions of kindness are revealed through the way they complement and compliment my work, my life, my family, and my kindness toward them.

We tend to underestimate the positive impact of compliments. As a result, we don't give as many as we should. The compliment is one of those powerful, small actions that brighten your day and someone else's day.

The only cost is the time to observe and respond. My incredible colleague, Tina Boogren, taught me this lesson. Compliments are a core strength of hers. We worked together for two days while writing this book. Tina passes out compliment cards from time to time, and she discreetly left a card for me on my chair. It said:

Tim, it is always a gift to be in the room with you; I always learn so much, and I'm filled with "JOY," thanks to you. So grateful. #LYBL, Tina (smiley face)

I have been doing this work for a long time, and yet, I was floating on air. It felt so *good* to receive a compliment in the middle of a workday.

Why are compliments so impactful? The act helps us feel valued and respected by others, to feel like we *belong*. When we get a compliment, it gives us feedback about what other people think of us. We feel significantly better after both giving and receiving a compliment compared to how we felt beforehand.[99]

So, I have a springtime kindness experiment for you. Consider adapting Tina's kindness action by creating and passing out compliment cards to your students and colleagues until the end of spring. Make it part of your *finishing well* this season of the school year. Print them or just write them on note cards. Maybe sign them and add a smiley face (I always do).

On the back of the cards, be specific with a few details. Details can elevate a so-so compliment to a great one, so make it a point to highlight specific qualities or actions. If giving compliments is a bit out of character for you, lean into it anyway.

Then, for six weeks, pass them out. A lot of them. Be generous.

Don't worry; you can't overdo compliments—as an act of kindness, they are infinite. However, be sure you mean what you say, that they feel connected to your personality, and that they are not comparing a student or colleague to others.

Also, compliment strangers you encounter outside of school, such as the barista at your local coffee shop, the restaurant waitress, the grocery store clerk, and more.

Here is a list of kindness and compliment samples for you to use at work!

- "You handled that difficult situation so well! Thank you!"
- "Your willingness to go the extra mile is appreciated. Thank you!"
- "I am so impressed by your ability to work well under pressure. Thank you!"
- "I love the way you bring out the best in your students (or colleagues)! Thank you!"
- "Your teaching today was brilliant! Thank you!" (Alternative: "Your *learning* today was brilliant.")

As you complete the MY Joy section, invite a trusted colleague to join you in the compliment experiment, and then compare joy notes!

MY JOY

Keep track of the number of compliment cards you give out this spring. Make cards using the suggestions provided or create your own.

When you finish your kindness/compliment experiment, reflect on how it went. Did it have an impact on your daily mood? Did it seem to increase your sense of joy at work? Or not? Explain in the following space.

One last thought. What should you do if you receive a compliment from a student or colleague? Simple. Say, "Thank you, that means a lot." Embrace it. Don't diminish it. Then go out and live a life of no regrets. That connection to joy is next.

SPRING

Regrets

The negative emotion of regret reveals the positive path for living.

—Daniel Pink

Let's dive right into that unpleasant emotion called regret. I'll start. Then it's your turn.

While preparing to write this book, a colleague interviewed me about the topic of educator wellness. Near the end of the interview, my colleague surprised me with this question: "What are your biggest regrets, professionally, so far?"

I was a bit stunned, as the question assumed I had regrets, and I felt vulnerable—all in a flash. It felt like minutes, but I am sure it was only seconds. I finally broke the silence.

My first regret was on my mind because I had just finished discussing the importance of physical-wellness routines based on how well we demonstrate positive food, movement, and sleep routines during the seasons of the school year. So, my first response was to say I regretted my decisions to completely ignore my physical-wellness routines for four years. Result: heart attack.

I regretted thinking I could do it all too. Husband, father, teacher, leader, student, coach, writer, traveler, faith follower, homeowner, community member, softball player . . . I stopped. In that moment of listing many of the roles I played in life, including the ones I didn't do very well, I realized my real regret.

I had been spinning a lot of plates. Many of which I still spin now. And because of my penchant for living a hurried life, I often failed at being kind, thoughtful, aware, compassionate, generous, grateful, self-reflective, on time, and connected to family and friends who I love. I spit these words out.

I took a deep breath, shocked at my deep-seated sense of failure, of not being enough, for my students, my colleagues, my friends, and most of all, my family members.

I had one other regret but did not share it with my colleague. I had sent an email to several colleagues in which my tone and words were terse, overblown, and too intense for the seriousness of the issue. Worse, the person who bore the brunt of my criticism was not the one responsible for the situation. That person was merely the messenger.

Yes, I thought. I do, indeed, have regrets.

Regret is a fundamental aspect of being *human*. *Regret*, as in, "to lament . . . to feel sorry or dissatisfied about."[100] Of course, there will be moments when we will feel like we don't quite measure up to the positive connections and communications we crave. *If only I had done more of the right thing or reached out more often, or . . . whatever.* Our profession demands we be kinder and more aware of others, right?

Our regrets fall into two categories: (1) those of action and (2) those of inaction.[101]

In the discussion with my colleague, I focused mostly on my *inaction*. My inaction toward eating, moving, and sleeping *well.* My inaction (or failure, as I referred to it that day) to be more kind, grateful, aware, and so on. We are more likely to regret what we didn't do throughout the seasons of our school years than what we did do. Regrets of inaction last longer than regrets of action because they reflect greater perceived opportunity.[102]

This school year has been a year of opportunity. And you are on the cusp of the final month. It is not too late to act on any regrets of inaction, of opportunities you did not take during this school year. The quote by Daniel Pink in this chapter's epigraph rings true.

Regret does indeed reveal a positive path forward. Since 2002, my food, movement, and sleep routines have drastically improved—a positive path forward.

The following is my personal list of *inaction* regrets (what I could have done more of) attached to my positive path forward.

- *Be kind:* Led to more compliment-giving.
- *Be thoughtful:* Led to improved consideration and awareness of others.
- *Be aware:* Led to noticing others more.
- *Be compassionate:* Led to more actions to relieve others' suffering.
- *Be generous:* Led to compartmentalizing my time and being more fully present with others.
- *Be grateful:* Led to more morning quiet time to become centered and prepared for my day.
- *Be self-reflective:* Led to more time spent sitting in silence, away from the noise of life.
- *Be punctual:* Led to . . . I am still working on this one!
- *Be connected to family and friends:* Led to more intentionality at *initiating* contact, emails, texts, dinners, travel, or events, such as an early Friday morning breakfast with a new friend or a weekly Thursday late-afternoon phone call with my eldest daughter.

Additionally, take time to look back on your possible regrets of *action*, such as my email issue. Do you need to apologize to someone? If yes, do it *now*! Don't delay.

Have at it. Don't be shy. What you regret will reveal what you value the most, and help you focus on future actions.

MY JOY

Think through your experiences since the start of this school year. List any regrets you have in the far-left column. Once you complete your list, decide which type of regret each one is—inaction or action—and place a checkmark in the appropriate column. Use the space to write about how you will respond to each regret as a positive way forward. Do you need to do more of something (a regret in the inaction column), or do you need to apologize (a regret in the action column)?

When you're finished, share your list with a trusted colleague and discuss, as appropriate.

Regrets	Inaction Regret	Action Regret

Regrets	Inaction Regret	Action Regret

You are now close to your final month of the spring season. Late April and May offer a time for understanding the possibilities ahead. A time for celebration and joy. That's next!

SPRING

Zotheka

Start by doing what's necessary; then do what's possible; and suddenly you are doing the impossible.

—St. Francis of Assisi

My son has a tattoo on his left arm. It says, "Let go." Tattoos are often a very personal and emotional representation of what we value, what matters to us most. For him, it is his daily reminder to live his life with *gezellig* (calm and cozy) when things get intense at work or at home.

And now, surprisingly, I am thinking of getting one too.

Mostly because of Savannah Guthrie.

In her book, *Mostly What God Does: Reflections on Seeking and Finding His Love Everywhere*, she opens with a story about her decision to get her first tattoo ever, at age 51. The tattoo on her arm simply says, "All my love," using her father's handwriting from a love letter her father wrote to her mother when they were first dating (courting). Her father had died when Savannah was sixteen, and the letters were discovered many years later.[103]

Savannah's story moved me. It felt to me like a story of possibilities, of connection. Also of love, yes, but of something so meaningful to her that she would stamp it in ink on her arm! It made me wonder, "What is important enough to you, meaningful enough in your life, something you once thought impossible, that you would stamp in ink on *your* body?"

What is something that holds special meaning for you? It might be a tattoo, letter, photograph, symbol, collection, keepsake, journal, special place, and so on.

_____
_____
_____
_____
_____
_____
_____
_____
_____
_____
_____
_____
_____
_____
_____
_____
_____
_____
_____
_____

While writing this chapter, my wife and I were part of a celebration of life for the father of two of our neighbors. They are brother and sister and, along with their respective spouses, have been close personal friends of ours for several years. We are fortunate to be part of a community of friends that bring joy into daily life experiences outside of work.

Their father had lived a full life, living well into his nineties. He, his wife, three children, and four grandchildren all grew up in our community. They had a way of adopting people into the family circle, which operated more like a horseshoe and less like an enclosed circle.

The celebration of life was held in the backyard of his home, and the place was packed. All ages, shapes, and sizes. Many of the celebrations were filled with funny or tearful memories, stories of how he made an impact on their life journey.

I had the benefit of being an observer, witnessing these stories of love and action, lessons learned, and lessons earned. The coming together, the energy of these friends, and the connection of memories and manifestos did not escape me.

Many stories were about moments of adventure and support. This father and grandfather seemed to be a possibility thinker. His life embodied a sense of questioning what is possible as a way of overcoming the impossible. He often used the French phrase *pourquoi pas*, meaning, "Why not?"

There was some heavy lifting required to prepare the place for such an event and then do the teardown afterward. Celebrations do end. We say what we want to say and eventually head home. The memories, though, always linger.

Several family members and close friends had pitched in, rowing the boat together during the weeks-long preparation, carrying the day forward, and then cleaning up. Later that evening, they gathered to share words of kindness, gratefulness, deep love, and joy for the celebration of *now* and how it connected to possibilities for the *future*. The posterity of life from one generation to the next was palpable.

It made me feel so alive. Sometimes, when you see the sheer joy shining inside and outside of people you love, in moments like this, it lifts your heart and reminds you how the impossible can become possible if you just do what is necessary one day, one event, one memory at a time. And remember to ask, "Why not?"

I know what you are most likely thinking: What does my story have to do with tattoos, and what's up with the chapter title, *Zotheka* (pronounced *zoe-TAY-kuh*)? Well, *zotheka* is the whole point of my future tattoo.

Malawi is a landlocked, mostly rural country along the East African Rift Valley in Southeast Africa. I first read about the country when we visited our youngest daughter in Tanzania during her Peace Corps assignment. Malawi is a western neighbor. *Zotheka* comes from the Chewa language, a primary language spoken in Malawi, and roughly translates to "It's possible!"[104]

While preparing to write this book, I wanted to write a chapter about overcoming the impossible by taking steps to make certain hope-filled outcomes of our work life possible. We are future role models for our students and colleagues. We are *why not* thinkers, correct?

The following are some examples of making the seemingly impossible possible.

- The preK–12 curriculum seems impossible to learn for many of our students, and yet we design lessons every day to *make it possible* to learn and ask, *why not?*
- Many of our students suffer from achievement gaps, and catching them up seems impossible, and yet we offer interventions, support services, and counseling and do not give up. We make *closing the achievement gap possible* and ask, *why not?*
- Many of our students are disengaged from the day-to-day life in the classroom. Engaging them in classroom life seems impossible, and yet we do not give up. We make *classroom engagement and enjoyment possible* and ask, *why not?*
- Many of our colleagues work in isolation and have given up. We advocate for systemic change and collaboration with colleagues to create a more equitable, flexible, responsive, and

student-centered learning environment. We do not give up. We make *eradicating workplace isolation possible* and ask, *why not?*

- Many of our colleagues experience high levels of stress. By prioritizing self-care, seeking support from colleagues and mentors, and promoting well-being, we build resilience to stress and sustain our commitment to students and each other. We do not give up. We make *our well-being routines possible* and ask, *why not?*

MY JOY

With one month to go, think about last fall and the start of the school year. What part of your work life with students and colleagues seemed impossible then but now, because of your individual and *collective* effort, is possible?

_____
_____
_____
_____
_____
_____
_____
_____
_____

How will you collectively celebrate overcoming your *it's not possible* barrier as this school year nears its end?

_____
_____
_____
_____
_____
_____
_____
_____
_____

What about my tattoo, you ask? Well, the rest of that joy story comes from knowing how to tell *your* professional life story. That joy creation is next!

SPRING

Commuovere

The stories people tell have a way of taking care of them. If stories come to you, care for them.

—Barry Lopez

As May begins, the finish line is in sight. Can you see it? What will be the heartwarming story you tell *this* school year? What will be your *commuovere*?

Yes, *commuovere* (pronounced *kom-MWOH-veh-reh*) is another one of those untranslatable words to English like *gezellig* and *zotheka*. It is Italian and loosely translates to the emotion or feeling of having been moved in a heartwarming way by a story told by another. It is my hope that a few of the stories throughout this book have connected for you and touched your heart professionally or personally.

There is a formula for telling a good story. I will share a story from a spring season moment in my professional life. I will then share the components of a great story and challenge you to write your own story about this school year, if you choose. Ready?

"It's impossible. You will never be able to do it. Just let it go. You don't know our kids. You are setting them up for failure. There is no classroom space I can give you."

My assistant principal spoke these words to me at the high school where I worked. It was my ninth season of teaching, and I had been hired three years earlier to boost participation in our honors mathematics program, create an Advanced Placement calculus course, and inspire more students to enroll in college preparatory mathematics classes. I had put in a request to create a mathematics competition team and asked for classroom space to run our practices before and after school.

My response to my assistant principal was to show up to the next school board meeting with three of my best students and speak with the board members. We stated our case that academic competitions were just as worthy as athletic competitions. Moreover, I reminded our board members that a single helmet for the freshman football team (at that time) cost $72. I was only asking for ten helmets to fund this new program. Seemed reasonable to me.

And so, we got started.

But it wasn't easy. Our mathematics competitions were like track meets—multiple events that lasted three to four hours. We had single events for specific mathematics subjects and grade levels. We also had relay events, and two-, four-, and eight-person team events. Finally, we had calculator events and oral presentation events about college-level mathematics content. Results from these events would be added up for a total score. The breadth of competition required a lot of students to participate—ideally, somewhere in the mid-twenties.

In the beginning, we showed up at a local or regional competition with a team of eight to ten students. We scored a lot of zeros for certain events as we had no entrants available. These meets were held on Thursday evenings or Saturdays, which created conflicts for students who were also in band, sports, or had responsibilities at home.

In the beginning, we placed last in most of our mathematics competitions. Occasionally, I would get an "I told you so" from the assistant principal. However, my mindset was always that we would make the impossible possible for the students participating. They were on fire for the preparation and the reward of learning, so I was too. A few students were receiving college scholarship offers. In our high-poverty school, these offers made a difference.

Our spring season ended with a Saturday competition of twenty-three schools. We finished nineteenth with eleven students. Several of the other school coaches shared their ideas and materials with me regarding how to recruit students and prepare them for future competitions.

Two years later, at that end-of-season competition, we had a team of twenty-nine students in the auditorium as the results were announced. The judges announced the top ten schools, starting with the team finishing tenth. We thought we might be tenth or ninth.

As we sat there anxiously awaiting the results, I reflected on how we got there. We had tripled the number of students that had access to our honors-level programs. We specifically recruited more girls to the team, making it more acceptable to be smart in mathematics and science. We held yearlong practices on Saturday afternoons, studying and learning together, as various parents rotated hosting our team at their homes. We were able to secure academic elective credit for participating on our team and help graduates receive scholarship support as local businesses provided funding for the program.

As they announced tenth, ninth, and eighth places, I didn't hear our school's name and started to worry. I knew we had done well, maybe tenth at best. I knew there was no guarantee that hard work would pay off with some reward. I was preparing my speech to let my team know how proud I was of them, even if we did not get a trophy.

The announcements continued: "In seventh place, school X... in sixth place, school Y... in fifth place, *West Chicago Community High School District 94!*" The entire place erupted. We were screaming, hugging, and going crazy. Fellow coaches who knew our journey stood up and applauded.

And the best part? Our four captains who went onstage to accept the trophy were remarkably diverse. Those students made the impossible possible.

A good story is a blend of the following ingredients.

- *Persons:* The people who figure into the story
- *Obstacles:* The problem the people are trying to solve
- *Actions:* What the people plan to do and then *do*
- *Cause and effect:* The effects (intended or unintended) of carrying out the actions
- *Context and surprise:* Details surrounding the people, actions, and the unexpected

I will leave it to you to determine whether my end-of-year story passed this litmus test! Now it is time to write your own *commuovere* story. Use the space on the next page.

MY JOY ♥

Write or share verbally your best heartwarming story for this school season that is about to end. Use the five guidelines to tell your good story as you see fit. If possible, before the school year ends, share your story with others too. Maybe tell your students, colleagues, or team. It will bring them joy and engage them in the journey they have been on with you as their leader.

_____

Most likely, your story reveals the effort and collective perseverance that carried you through this year. As you enter the final days of *this* school year, it is time to pursue your *meraki*. Next!

SPRING

Meraki

> *The most joyful are those who make the time and exercise the most creativity every day.*
>
> —Georgina Rivera

We are artisans. We live inside a creative life. Would you agree?

As such, this school year has been another creation. One more attempt at a masterpiece with this group of students, colleagues, and parents. You saw the promise of the school year's debut back in August, and now the story has been told. That fall season debut was poised with expectations for how everything would turn out—and that previously unwritten reality has now been written. It is staring you in the face. May always arrives. No takebacks.

Whether this has been your first attempt at creating a great school year for students and colleagues or your thirtieth attempt, you have created *your* masterpiece. You have designed and taught and influenced your own master class in teaching and learning, so to speak.

As artisans, we have given our life away to a series of new beginnings, year after year. New chances to paint the canvas. We start over each year despite setbacks. We push forward through the doubt and sometimes despair that come with that winter season. We slog ahead despite the small voice in our heads that sometimes tells us to stop.

There are no awards given out because we recovered our confidence when others had doubts. In short, we write and create our own story anew, day after day. School season after school season. It is what silent heroes do.

We, too, are all different. We look different, our stories are different, our path to get to this part of May is different, our history is different, yet we share something in common.

Briefly describe how you poured yourself wholeheartedly into your creative canvas for student learning this school year. Describe the colleagues who are part of that canvas.

_____
_____
_____
_____
_____
_____
_____
_____
_____
_____
_____
_____
_____
_____
_____
_____
_____
_____
_____
_____

Our *meraki*.

Meraki (pronounced *meh-RAH-kee*) is a Greek word that roughly translates to the pouring of yourself wholeheartedly into something and doing it with soul, creativity, and love.[105] If you are giving your best (intellectually and emotionally) throughout the year, the end results will take care of themselves.

Our spirit of generosity toward students and colleagues and our collective perseverance as we show up day in and day out is more creative each day. We demonstrate a strange mix of dogged determination and wild hope—especially for the most disadvantaged who are part of this year's canvas.

I think the artisan life, the creative life, takes a lot of nerve, humility, and just enough self-confidence to believe we can make it. And here we are. On the doorstep of finishing our masterpiece for *this* school season. It's self-judgment time in a way. And there is only one way you should judge your artisan creation this school year.

As described in the previous chapter, it is *not* always about the results of your work life. Goals achieved, improved outcomes in student learning, and more are important. But not as important as the way your joyful heart led you, your students, and your colleagues *during* the journey.

MY JOY

So, what happened to Peter? When we discussed his story in Spring, Chapter 1: Finishing (early March, page 123), he was not creating a masterpiece year for sure. When we found him again in Spring, Chapter 5: Engagement (early April, page 139), he and I were having a conversation about engaging more wholeheartedly in his professional life. We were at the pancake house.

Peter's story is also my *meraki* story. The weekend before we met at the pancake house, I had a decision to make about how to handle the situation. On the one hand,

I wanted to condemn his choices. He was not throwing himself wholeheartedly into his work. Just the opposite. No *meraki* for him. I wanted to judge him and scream at him to get his act together. But rejection, in any form, can shatter someone's soul.

And if I judged him, if my approach was to condemn his behavior, then what kind of canvas was I painting this year as his coach and supervisor? What does that say about my artisanal integrity?

My self-judgment about how to provide Peter with honest feedback that was kind and thoughtful, yet firm, needed to be about what was in my heart. And my heart saw a person in a lot of pain. I derived no joy from holding up the proverbial mirror to his face.

The next day after our meeting, Peter and I met with Linda (not her real name), another teacher on our staff. He had offered up two solutions for moving forward and getting out of his rut, to paint a better canvas through the end of this school season and into the following one. He wanted to teach some different grade levels and courses. Linda was the only faculty member he was willing to work with.

As his director, I made both happen. Linda was a great teacher and a coach he would listen to and work with, and she taught one of the grade-level courses he was currently teaching and one he would move to the following school year. My only caveat was that he had to meet daily with Linda for the rest of the current school year and then once per week the following year. He would need to do summer work to learn the curriculum and become better prepared to paint a stronger canvas next year. I would be his teacher for the summer, and we set our dates for working together. Peter's students needed him to recapture *the him* from his younger years.

He retired three school seasons later. And once again, we went to the same pancake house. Remember step 4 from Spring, Chapter 2: Acknowledging Joy (page 127)? I wrote him a one-page letter. Something I did for all retirees who worked with me. I read him the letter and then gave him a copy. It was hard for him to turn around his bitterness so quickly. Yet, he gave it his best *meraki*. He made the effort to pour himself wholeheartedly back into the task of teaching. He finished those final three school seasons better. And as I often reminded him, in the end, *only you can judge you.*

In our work life, we walk the high wire between discernment and judgment. That wire sits high in the air, supported by what is in our hearts.

Only you can judge you. Be truthful. Be kind. Be positive. Be patient. Remember that innate neurological circuitry of your mind poses a very real challenge: positive stimuli tend to roll through it while negative stimuli get flagged, captured, and deferred to. But you can consciously override those tendencies in simple and effective ways each day by focusing on positive experiences, valuing them, and helping them sink in.

Focus on your *meraki* for this school season, and joy will be there on the other side.

MY JOY

The concept of *meraki* is part of the Greek culture, with an emphasis on a thoughtful, heartfelt passion and appreciation of small things.

Write about a few small actions you took this school season that made a positive difference for you, your students, or your colleagues and became part of your creative masterpiece this school year.

_____
_____
_____
_____
_____
_____
_____
_____
_____
_____
_____
_____
_____
_____
_____
_____
_____
_____
_____

Memorial Day is just around the corner. It is time for *your* valedictory address before the summer season kicks into high gear. That's next!

SPRING

Valedictory

Goodbyes are only for those who love with their eyes. Because for those who love with heart and soul, there is no such thing as separation.

—Rumi

We are nearing the end of May now. Graduation and other year-end celebrations are closing in. We made it! Another school season of our professional lives can get checked off the calendar. It is time to say goodbye. Beginnings and endings are like that. We prepare our hellos and goodbyes.

Part of the melancholy feeling at this time of the year is about the separation experience between you, your students, and your colleagues. You invested so much time and effort into their growth over the past ten months. Some students will leave your elementary building and go to middle school. Are they ready? Some will leave your middle school building and go to high school. *Thank goodness*, you might think but most likely won't say it out loud! Still, others are graduating from high school and leaving you for a bigger, more wide-open world. Scary. Exciting.

Can there be joy in saying goodbye? Are you so exhausted you can't feel the joy of a job well done in this season of your professional life? Take a closer look at the epigraph offered by Rumi. The truth is, we are never truly separated from the impact we have on those students entrusted to us, for good or for bad.

Their lives are forever intersected with ours.

The joy is not so much in the goodbye as it is in knowing we loved them with our heart and soul. After all, our work is transformative for others, is it not? It's just that the *knowing* of our impact is often delayed.

Write a celebration note to yourself. List a transformative moment, a victory with students or colleagues that was joyful for you this school year.

_____
_____
_____
_____
_____
_____
_____
_____
_____
_____
_____
_____
_____
_____
_____
_____
_____
_____
_____
_____
_____
_____
_____

♥ MY JOY

The word *valedictory* is an adjective used to describe something related to or serving as a farewell. It often refers to a speech, address, or message given as a farewell, typically by someone leaving a position, graduating, or departing from a group or organization.[106] A valedictory speech is intended to express gratitude, reflect on experiences, and offer well-wishes to the audience or recipients. The term *valedictory* is derived from the Latin word *valedicere*, which means "to say farewell."[107]

The idea of saying farewell to any of my school seasons has often left me wondering about my personal expressions of gratitude for that school season about to end. If I was saying farewell to my job at the end of this year, what actions would show up in a personal valedictory address given to my work and effort?

How would I like to be remembered by my students and colleagues based on my work during *this* school season? I pared down my personal brainstorming list from twelve criteria to these four. You may have a different list, and that's OK too.

1. *Gratitude expresser:* My appreciation for the opportunity to contribute to students' achievements and successes
   I may not have been able to help every student over the bar of expected student performance. Yet. Will I be remembered for helping students and colleagues outperform expectations because of my competence, confidence, effort, and relational skills?
2. *Storyteller:* My ability to illustrate my positive impact on students, colleagues, and the school community (I could see beyond myself)
   I know we learn through stories. I would like to think I was a hero maker for many of my students.[108] Will I be remembered for helping others find their own hero story?

3. *Collaborator:* My willingness to change, grow, and innovate new instructional and assessment routines with colleagues that enrich the learning environment for students

   Collaboration is hard. Yet it is worth it! Collaboration breaks down inequities unintentionally created by our private actions. Will I be remembered as someone you enjoyed as part of your team?

4. *Encourager:* My intention to continue making a positive impact

   I need this. Your words of support and confidence matter to me. They keep me going, school season in and school season out. Will I be remembered for my relentless attempts to inspire students and colleagues to not give up in their effort for growth and learning this year?

It is a good idea to give yourself a valedictory address at the end of each school year. Give yourself a heartfelt and sincere expression of appreciation and recognition of your contributions as you bid farewell to a long and hopefully worthwhile school season, despite the reality of hardships and adversity faced and overcome.

This time of year gives you an opportunity to celebrate achievements this season as part of your career as a whole. A school season you can never get back. You build your legacy as you walk it. Honor your walk this year and make time to express gratitude for your dedication to our noble profession, perhaps with a trusted colleague or your entire team.

MY JOY

Use this page to write your personal valedictory farewell address. Use the *how I will be remembered* prompts provided or create your own freestyle summary. When completed, take time to share your wisdom learned with a trusted colleague.

A sense of gratitude for my commitment to students' success

___
___
___
___
___
___
___
___
___
___
___
___
___
___

A story that illustrates my positive impact on students, colleagues, and the school community (I could see beyond myself)

A celebration of my willingness to change, grow, and innovate new routines with colleagues that enriched the learning environment for students

A feeling of encouragement because of my ability to continue making a positive impact

As we near the end of this school season, there is nothing quite like the final ceremony and how it represents the joy of *ubuntu*. That reality is next!

SPRING

Ubuntu

Whatever affects one directly affects all indirectly. I can never be what I ought to be until you are what you ought to be.
—Martin Luther King, Jr.

The word *ubuntu* (pronounced *oo-BOON-too*) has its roots in the Bantu languages of the Nguni people in Southern Africa, particularly in Zulu and Xhosa. It is a complex and multifaceted concept that encompasses various meanings. In a philosophical and cultural context, *ubuntu* is often translated as humanity toward others. *Ubuntu* is, in a way, a South African philosophy that recognizes how we, as humans, are bound together in ways we cannot see.[109]

I am what I am because of who we all are.

I stood on the stage in the Welsh-Ryan Arena at Northwestern University in Evanston, Illinois, and quietly scanned the crowd. Students, parents, grandparents, siblings, community members, and staff. Board members, certified faculty, and administrators were wearing their robes, stoles, and caps, highlighting their university colors and academic integrity. Security members were in uniform and in evidence. More than seven thousand people were gathered to begin our graduation and commencement ceremony.

All shapes and sizes, nationalities, religions, languages, and more were present. It was electrifying and eclectic in its beauty. People were standing and sitting with a quiet buzz around the pavilion as our underclass music students warmed up for the opening middle section stanza of Edward Elgar's "Pomp and Circumstance March in D Major, Op. 39, No. 1."

Although I was about to participate in one of my favorite events as a school superintendent, it was in that moment right before the ceremony that I felt this quiet joy from a job well done by so many in our school community over the past thirteen years. I felt this sense of *ubuntu* with the crowd. Everyone attending was about to see the fruits of their labor walk across the stage and receive their diplomas. We were indeed a group of humans bound together in ways we could and could not know or see.

Beginnings and endings flashed through my brain. We are who we are in *this* moment, this time, only because of all the moments that came before it. Past is prologue in our line of work, and the fruits of our *community of labor* were about to walk across the stage.

For sure, this was an ending for our 1,200-plus graduating seniors. And yet, it was their beginning too. Looking out at the sea of adult faces representing a wide range of ages, I felt this sense of interconnectedness with my community, as it had taken all of us to push and pull our graduates to this celebratory moment. *Ubuntu: I am what I am because of who we all are* was ringing in my ears.

There was an interconnected nature to our humanity in the room. In that moment, I felt like my individual well-being was tied to the well-being of everyone else in that arena, and part of my sense of purpose and worth would and could not exist without those in the room. *This culminating moment was exactly why I joined the profession*, I thought to myself. There was, for me, this brief sense of a harmonious society built on a long, thirteen-year battle of teaching and learning, counseling and caring, parenting and grandparenting, a coming together in *this* moment, in *this* time.

I also knew this was my last moment on that stage. I would be leaving a school community I had called home for twenty-three years. I felt this melancholy mix of joy and sadness. I would miss this moment of each year, fiercely. I knew this, deep in my bones and my brain. And yet, it was my time to yield to others. To let go. My final thought as "Pomp and Circumstance" began was *finish well*, followed by a quick overwhelming sense of gratefulness for it all. I let the music move me one last time. Then, it was time to stand and let the well-deserved community ceremony begin.

MY JOY

Ubuntu presents the idea that an individual's identity is inseparable from the community. The well-being of the community and the individual are intertwined, emphasizing a sense of shared destiny and purpose. Central to *ubuntu* is the notion of empathy and compassion. It encourages individuals to understand and feel the experiences of others, fostering a sense of solidarity toward the relief of suffering, similar to our journey in Winter, Chapter 6: Compassion (page 87).

Ubuntu places great value on social harmony and cooperation. It suggests that the good of the community is essential for the well-being of the individual and vice versa. Is this not the role we chose to serve when we signed up for our profession? Is this not the greater good and the greater reward for all our hard work and effort that began almost ten months ago and culminates in this final, shared experience?

Ubuntu implies a sense of collective responsibility for the welfare of the community. Individuals are encouraged to contribute positively to the common good. *Ubuntu* emphasizes the importance of treating others with respect and recognizing the inherent dignity of every individual. This contributes to the creation of a supportive and respectful social environment.[110]

The philosophy of *ubuntu* encourages peaceful conflict resolution and reconciliation. Much like our expectations in a well-functioning professional learning community, *ubuntu* promotes dialogue and understanding to resolve our differences.

As I looked out at the audience—seven thousand strong, at least for the next hour or so—differences would be set aside and momentarily resolved because of the common inspiration of this transitional moment achieved by the seventeen- and eighteen-year-old graduates entering the arena.

I watched as the multiple rows of our 1,200-plus graduates came marching in wearing their shoulder braids for academic achievement or community service hours.

Share a time in your life when a graduation ceremony or a personal celebration at the end of the school year brought joy to your life.

_____
_____
_____
_____
_____
_____
_____
_____
_____
_____
_____
_____
_____
_____
_____
_____
_____
_____
_____
_____
_____
_____
_____
_____
_____
_____
_____
_____

Some were solemn, others were laughing, some were waving, some were brave and perhaps scared, too. Graduation is like that. It brings out our love and our emotions for the work, for the people, and for the community.

∞

What I was feeling in that moment was the joy of *ubuntu*: *I find my meaning in you, and you find your worth in me.* This is, after all, what our profession *asks* of us. Season in and season out.

MY JOY

As this school season ends, describe a few genuine moments of joy you experienced through your specific contribution to the worth and well-being of the students, colleagues, and parents in the school community you serve.

_____

Like my moment in this story, for some of you, this is your final goodbye to our profession. A great question to ask as that goodbye moment arrives is, "How will you be remembered?" The surprising answer is next.

SPRING

13
Vanaprastha

If at some point in your life, you should come across anything better than justice, truth, self-control, courage—it must be an extraordinary thing indeed.

—Marcus Aurelius

Dear reader: I am writing this final chapter in part 3 different from the others. It is written as a dialogue between me and you as we approach the end of spring. Some of you are leaving the profession for the final time. This dialogue is for you. And for those of you who eventually follow. Your voice is in italics. Enjoy!

Vanaprastha

Well. It is over.

You bagged, tagged, and dragged your stuff.

The boxes are in your car.

It's only for a few months.

You'll be back to start another school season soon.

This time, I am not coming back.

What's that you just said?

This is my vanaprastha.

You're retiring into the forest?

No, not literally.

Ah. Your life goals are just readjusting.

You get it now.

This is your final goodbye. To *this* life.

Yes.

Do you think you made a difference?

I'm not sure, to be honest.

Want me to help you decide?

Sure, it's the last time we will talk, most likely.

There is a downside to knowing.

That's OK; it's too late anyway.

That part will be up to you. Ready?

Yes.

You have had a lot of professional successes, recognition, and accomplishments.

Thank you.

But those virtues do not matter.

What? Why not?

It is not how we will remember you. Three, five, ten, twenty-five years from now.

That makes me sad. How will I be remembered?

Your eulogy virtues.

What are those?

Character qualities we remember about you when you are gone for good.

Kindness, compassion, integrity, courage, wisdom, justice, self-control, generosity.

I get your point. Is it too late?

Maybe for your students and colleagues, but not for others.

The creatures of your new forest—your new life goals—are waiting for you.

I'm tired. Will they wait?

Yes. Don't wait too long.

It's never too late for you, and them, to benefit from an extraordinary you.

Spring:
A Season to Show Resolve
Your Conclusions

During this spring season, which of the joy actions in Spring chapters 1–13 about *finishing well* most resonate with your current personal and professional joy journey? In reflection, what are three to five brief takeaways about growing strong during the spring season of this school year?

--- **MY** J O Y ♥ ---

Write about your favorite takeaways from this spring season that might serve your overall joy journey as an educator and your well-being as you transition from the exhaustion of finishing well and transition into the summer months and a much-needed time of rest and recreation!

_____
_____
_____
_____
_____
_____

You can check out my video here as I provide my conclusions and insight from Part 3: Spring—A Season to Show Resolve. Thanks for joining the spring journey with me. It was emotional, for sure!

PART 4

SUMMER:
A SEASON TO REJUVENATE

Growing Strong in a Season of Rest

You made it. Another full school year has come and gone. It most likely felt heavy at times and joyful at others. You felt the weight of the responsibility to be your best every day. You felt the challenge and positive impact of your life on students and colleagues. You have thank-you notes from parents, students, and colleagues to prove it.

You were a steward for the success of every student entrusted to you, and they, in turn, are the beneficiaries of your joy pursuits. Your daily and weekly efforts in this past school year allowed you to move closer to living your best life each day within a profession that serves your greater purpose. They, and you, must move on. Another school year awaits in just a few short months!

But first, you get to rest. The summer sun and the warm embrace of June and July. The hours of daylight provide time to unwind, explore, and spend quality time with others.

It's a season to reset, let go of the past school year, enjoy your relationships, and reconnect with your purpose before you transition to the next school year in late summer. You plot your joy path for the new school season ahead, while the pace slows, and you have time to reflect on the past school year to focus on future improvements.

June is a time to give your brain a break and enjoy a slower pace of daily life. Take time to deepen your bonds with friends and family members you love, through vacation activities, quiet moments at home, late-night summer sunsets, and the creation of lasting memories with those you love.

July offers a chance to recharge and invest more deeply in your personal life and friendships, deepen relationships that spark improved professional joy, and find space during a slower pace to stretch and grow.

August looms around the corner, of course. August signals the mental and emotional stress of transition. Summer will be ending, and fall isn't too far away. A new school year is about to begin, and joy will not happen without attention and intention. The anticipation gnaws at you a little bit. Can you preserve the joy, peace, and pace of summer and carry it with you into the beauty of fall and all it represents? You wonder. You doubt. You hope. You prepare.

But first, you *rest*.

SUMMER

Rest

To rest is to regenerate, to take a break is to gain strength.
—Lailah Gifty Akita

Thank goodness for the summer season ahead!

A time to rest, finally. Rest is essential to a joyful life. Rest is more than sleep. Sleep is a time to recover from your physical exhaustion. Rest is the way we recover from our psychological exhaustion as we take breaks away from the high-cognitive-demand tasks of work and home. Rest is found in the short daily breaks and longer weekly breaks of the low-cognitive-demand variety that are inherently enjoyable.[111]

Our brains need a *daily* break. A rest period where we just zone out—not by scrolling through social media posts on our phone, but by getting away from the noise of the constant inputs of information coming at us. By allowing our brain to be *rested* each day, our sleep quality is better, chronic pain is diminished, work productivity is enhanced, and our overall life satisfaction is greater. Rest strengthens our brain, which enhances learning.[112]

MY JOY

During this past school year, describe how you intentionally took daily or weekly rest breaks away from the intense noise of work and home.

_____
_____
_____
_____
_____
_____
_____
_____
_____
_____
_____
_____
_____

The benefits are bountiful.

So, why do we push rest and the idea of intentional breaks to the bottom of our daily, weekly, and monthly to-do lists? Why is it so hard to find meaningful rest? The chapters that follow are designed to help you with the summer season of rest and will endure to serve you well into the fall of your next school season.

One caution, as you fill your summer life with lots of exciting, action-packed days and weekends—your time off from the school season can be just as depleting and demanding as the energy drain during the season. Be sure to take good doses of detachment from your devices and your work. Take a solid week or two *completely off*, and practice *deep play* (hobbies or sports you might enjoy with others—like my softball buddies from Fall, Chapter 2: Remember, page 11). So, get plenty of sleep and movement. Every day. Your brain will thank you!

In Fall, Chapter 1: Beginnings (page 7), I describe the start of the first year of my second job as a teacher. The job where I started the school year on a nine-day strike.

I did not yet know anyone on the faculty or staff. A veteran teacher named Sarah (not her real name) reached out, as we were teaching many of the same mathematics classes. We struck up a friendship a few weeks after the strike. I asked her if she wanted to join me for lunch in my room rather than an often-negative faculty cafeteria area.

Every day during fifth period, at 11:55 a.m., Sarah walked over to my room (212) from her room (210), and we sat in a couple of student desks and chatted about life, music, home, family, and more. Occasionally, we would talk about work, but not very often. Our lunch "hour" (actually, twenty-eight minutes) together lasted through the end of the school year.

When our schedules came out for the next year, Sarah and I once again had the same lunch period. A good brain-break rest within our intense days. That next school year started, and Sarah was a no-show to my room for lunch. Things got busy as they always do at the start of the school year. Eventually, I wandered over to her room.

Sarah was at her desk eating lunch, and there were twelve students sitting in desks practicing mathematics and occasionally getting help from her and each other. These students had the same lunch as Sarah, so she had offered to help them.

I thought this was such a good idea that I started to do the same with my students. Any student with a free fifth period who wanted extra help could eat lunch in my room. Eventually, the place was packed as I provided snacks as well. In some ways, it was fun. But it was also exhausting. No rest.

I got to the end of the year, summer (my season of rest) was approaching, and my emotional tank was nearly empty. Empty for my own young toddlers at home, empty for teaching summer school, empty for preparing lessons for next year, empty for a vacation. Empty for my friendships and colleagues in our building. I was thirty-two years old and very tired.

And then I made it worse. We needed the money, so I said *yes* to teaching two summer school sessions and coaching summer basketball camps. I was at the school every day, and then it was suddenly opening day for my tenth season of teaching. I was exhausted, *and* I was about to enter the marathon of a new school year. I did not stand a chance.

Sure enough, Sarah came to my rescue. She said that, as a veteran teacher (at least more veteran than me), she could not once again give up her "duty-free" lunch. Could we have our lunch break together again this year? I concurred. Isn't that what *duty-free* means?

Relaxing and taking a break is not a waste of your time. It is an investment in your well-being. Breaks reset your attention and incubate new ideas. Rest is both a source of joy and a path to mastery.[113] Breaks help sustain your passion for the work by reducing fatigue and raising energy (a burnout preventer of sorts). My lunch with Sarah regenerated my brain power and my energy tank.

Breaks unlock fresh ideas and boost creativity for the tasks of the day.[114] I often find my most creative space while on my forty-five-minute run. And breaks deepen our learning. Taking a brief break enhances our ability to recall information into memory.[115]

What kind of rest breaks do you need? The following are three suggestions to help you throughout the school year and especially during the summer season.

- *Time-off breaks:* Summer season! A complete break away from your work life. Real summer rest should not be task oriented, but rather freeing and meaningful to you. Spending time in nature, listening to music, taking a family vacation, strolling along the beach, and reading for leisure are examples of real rest.

- *Daily rest breaks:* What you do and when you do it during the day matter less than *how* the break activity makes you *feel*. If it feels like drudgery, that is *not* good. If it brings you joy—like quiet time at a picnic table, nature walks in the winter, my lunchtime discussions with Sarah, or playing softball with my buddies at night during the school year—then it is restorative.
- *Family and friends breaks:* Find activities you enjoy. Don't always go it alone! At times, invite others to join you for a hike or for non-work-related activities, such as volunteering, vacationing, and conversations. Breaks often become more meaningful and memorable when they *include others*.

MY JOY

Use this space to write about your favorite summer-season rest activities.

Time-off breaks: What are your plans for long-term rest breaks (either by yourself or with others) this summer?

_____
_____
_____

Daily rest breaks: How will you take daily rest breaks this summer *and* during the fall, winter, and spring seasons?

_____
_____
_____

Family and friends breaks: Who would you most like to take rest breaks with this summer, at work or outside of work? Have you told them? When will you meet to discuss a brain-rest plan for the next school year (fall, winter, and spring seasons) ahead?

_____
_____
_____

Each day, we should enjoy our work life and help others enjoy theirs as well. Without joy, our real potential stays hidden. Our summer season of rest gives us the space, place, and pace to reminisce and embrace pleasurable events, ensuring we enter the next season with a full, high-energy emotional tank. That is next.

SUMMER

Reminisce

Sometimes you will never know the value of a moment until it becomes a memory.

–Dr. Seuss

Before this past school year and the fall, winter, and spring seasons get too far away, you should *reminisce* over the most *positive* moments you experienced at work or at home during this past school season.

When we reminisce, we recall short-term and long-term memories—our remembered experiences during those fall, winter, and spring seasons. *Reminiscing* is the process or practice of thinking or talking about your past experiences.[116]

MY JOY

Reminiscing is an action. We indulge briefly in the recollection of past events, particularly those that are positive or meaningful. We reflect, write, or talk about experiences, memories, and moments from the past. When you reminisce, you often recount positive stories and details about events that happened last school season with a sense of nostalgia and emotion.

While writing this chapter, a younger colleague was at dinner with some of our professional friends and

Write a list of moments based on your more *positive* experiences and accomplishments this past school year.

_____
_____
_____
_____
_____
_____
_____
_____
_____
_____
_____
_____
_____
_____
_____
_____
_____

texted me that they were reminiscing about old times! The nostalgia was palpable. Her text was eerily good timing!

Why reminisce? Because all your hard work of remembering and connecting to others from the most recent fall season, your heavy-lifting efforts of the past winter, and your attempts to finish well the previous spring season will quickly fade away, merging into prior years' experiences.

Also, positive reminiscence enhances your emotional resilience by increasing activity in brain regions associated with reward and reducing activity in stress-related areas.[117] Thus, positive reminiscence helps you recover from the emotional and physical exhaustion of the recently completed school year. Reminiscing is a joy choice as you share your stories.

We tend to get a reminiscence bump from ages fifteen to thirty.[118] The following story is a summary from my journal notes the summer after my sixth season of teaching (when I was twenty-eight years old).

The small farm community was so humbling for me. I did not know the difference between soybeans and baked beans. Field corn and sweet corn, beef cattle and dairy cows, and so much more. I did not know how to repair a fence, keep rats out of the henhouse, or put up or tear down a pole barn (or know what a pole barn was). And I had never shoveled manure. I had a lot to learn.

And yet, I loved the physical labor of the work. The smell and the action of baling and stacking hay, the smell of baked bread and apple pies. All the food! Literally farm to table. I am still amazed by the incredible challenge of farming, and I'm so grateful to the community that let me in and taught me (a teacher of their children) about farming and rural life.

It wasn't always smooth. I wanted every student to be prepared to go to college. Not all parents wanted that same goal. As a basketball coach, there were many community members who screamed and swore at me to play this player or that player. In the words of one of my respected reviewers for this book, they were joy vampires! I learned how to shut out the noise of negativity to find joy in my coaching life.

I worked with some exceptional colleagues. I remember their first names mostly. And I did not write down their last names. I suppose I thought I might always remember them. There was Jim (my roommate), Paula, Dave, Neil, Neal, Bob, Rich, Diane, and Glenn. Colleagues who wanted to share joy and lean into joy moments together. They taught me lessons of kindness toward others. Always.

Glenn and I played a lot of softball together, and he reminded me to keep a little distance from my work life. To seek balance and not let my life get consumed by the job. He was, of course, a school counselor.

My best memory of those joy moments from those summer seasons? Evening drives near dusk, the cool summer air, the incredible sweet smell of newly mown hay, and the sunset signaling the end of another day I could not not take back.

The strategies illustrated in my story can help you connect to positive actions and experiences toward joy. You will notice a few themes that serve my joy path through the skill of reminiscing, be it one day, one week, one season, or one full school year at a time.

- *Live with humility:* The farming life was hard, and yet there was a deep respect for the hard work required and the strong relationships with students' families and community members that emphasized collaboration and mutual respect.
- *Negativity cannot win:* No matter how hard you try to promote joy in others, some people prefer to take their negative emotions out on you or suck the joy out of you (the joy vampires). There were many times I had to tune out the noise from those seeking to destroy my joy.
- *Friends are a precious commodity:* Treat them in a mutually nourishing way, and only let in those who want to build joy into your life and be genuinely happy for you.
- *Kindness is a full-time job:* As I wrote in Spring, Chapter 6: Kindness (page 143), kindness is a primary way to walk through a joy-chosen life.
- *The job isn't everything:* It's great to throw yourself into your work, your students, and your colleagues. However, it is a losing proposition unless you promise to give yourself the gift of interests outside of work. Do not jeopardize the support of your family and friends.

As you reminisce about this past school season, complete the template (or use your own prompts) to keep a *reminiscence record* about your positive actions and experiences from this past school season.

I lived with humility. List some life hacks or tips you have learned about being confident, but humble.

_____
_____
_____
_____

Negativity did not win. When and how did you cultivate a positive and open heart in yourself and others?

___

My friends are a precious commodity. What advice would you give for developing closer work relationships?

___

My kindness was a full-time job. Write about one way you built kindness into your daily life.

___

The job wasn't everything. How did you give fully to your work life *and* stay balanced with time for home, solitude, and family?

___

So, seize this day; reminisce about the positive aspects of your professional and personal life. Stay engaged, stretched, and challenged as your tomorrows become your yesterdays and you take a serious break from the worry and concerns of the next season ahead.

SUMMER

Boketto

In quiet places, reason abounds.
—Adlai E. Stevenson

June is not only a season for rest and reflection, but also a time to stay away from the worry of the next season ahead. It is a time to let go of this past school season and give yourself a clean break from the overcrowded, noisy, and busy life you lead. Let your mind go wandering without much of a destination. There is a word for this:

Boketto (pronounced *boh-KEHT-toh*).

Boketto is a Japanese word that does not translate exactly into English but roughly describes the act of gazing vacantly into the distance without thinking about anything specific. It conveys a sense of serene contemplation or daydreaming, where you are lost in thought or simply enjoying the quiet and calm of the moment.[119]

Boketto beautifully captures a common, yet often overlooked, part of our human experience—mental relaxation. It can be refreshing for our mind to just go wandering for a while with no real destination or required focus. The pressures of the school year are off right now, and we should take advantage of it.

Engaging in *boketto* allows your mind to rest and wander freely without the pressure of focused thought. This mental relaxation reduces stress and anxiety, creating a sense of *gezellig* and well-being, which leads to joy.[120]

Although *boketto* involves a vacant gaze (which is how I must seem to my noneducator friends and family during the end of a school year or when writing a book), it encourages being present in the moment. This mindful presence heightens our awareness and appreciation of the surrounding environment, fostering a sense of contentment and joy.[121]

Describe your favorite summer season activity to let go of your work-life focus, take in your surroundings, and be fully present in the silence with no agenda.

_____
_____
_____
_____
_____
_____
_____
_____
_____
_____
_____
_____
_____
_____
_____
_____
_____
_____
_____

 # MY JOY

My *boketto* moments most often occur while I am immersed in and observing nature (see Fall, Chapter 5: Nature, page 23). Observing the sky, trees, mountains, water; city, urban, or rural landscapes. Connecting with nature enhances my mood and promotes feelings of appreciation and joy. There is always a sense of something way bigger than me in those moments of awe.

In hindsight, I did not take the time for very many *boketto* moments during my early years of teaching. I was too busy *doing* life to stop and be more observational, much less understand the joy benefits of just allowing my mind to be in a wandering, creative, and sometimes awestruck space.

And then, during June before my twentieth season of teaching, I got in my car and drove from Chicago to Montana. It had been a long school year for me. Both of my parents (my dad and my stepmom) had passed away, and now my "big as the Montana sky" colleague and friend was not doing well either. He had brain cancer. And he wanted me to come see him.

So, I did.

We spent several June days together, talking and laughing, despite how hard speech was for him now. We went fishing one day on a lake surrounded by mountainous landscapes. We did not catch much but sat in that boat for hours in the comfortable silence between two friends.

Writing about it now, more than thirty years later, there was a simplicity and a peace to it that defied why I was visiting him. *Boketto*, I suppose, embodies that simplicity and the beauty of doing nothing. Embracing this simplicity brought peace to both of us and deep, uncomplicated moments of joy that come from just *being*. This was not my normal day-in, day-out experience.

As we sat in the fishing boat, he asked me to give his eulogy when he passed away. He was very clear about what he wanted and needed me to say. It was why he had asked me to come see him. Outwardly, I said, "Of course." Inwardly, my feelings of sorrow were pulsating.

A few days later, it was time for me to leave. We said our goodbyes. This friend had shaped the direction of my life, and I was forever grateful. I got in my car, with no real hurry to get back home to Chicago, and decided to explore the various peaks that were part of the Rocky Mountain range running through Bozeman.

Within a few hours, while sitting on the back of my car, I allowed my mind to just wander and observe. I had an overwhelming sense of my own smallness. My own vulnerability. When you are in the presence of something vast and indescribable in its majesty, it's hard to maintain the view—and the voice in my head—that I was the center of the world. God felt ever-present to me. My Montana friend had asked me to ensure his eulogy would be centered on his faith. In his case, his walk and journey as a Christian man.

At that moment, thinking about my friend and my parents during this awe-inspiring sight, my problems at work, at home, and in life seemed minuscule. Diminished. Less intense. They seemed to shrink in size and importance. I felt a strange sense of relief, and for the first time in more than a year, I felt there was renewed hope for joy within the spiritual connection I sought for my life.

There are some wonderful joy benefits if you give yourself a few *boketto* moments this summer, and occasionally throughout each school season—fall, winter, and spring.

During *boketto* moments, your mind is free to drift, which can lead to creative thoughts and insights. Allowing your mind to wander without constraint provides an emotional release, letting go of your worries and tensions. This emotional freedom can contribute to a lighter, more joyful state of mind.

MY JOY

Use this space to write about a *boketto* moment during this summer season. Describe your *sense of serene contemplation or daydreaming where you are lost in thought or simply enjoying the quiet and calm* moment.

Where and when did, or will, it happen?

___

___

___

___

___

What benefits did or will you experience from allowing yourself to rest your brain from all the "doing" and action of the past ten months?

My *boketto* moment occurred while I was on a vacation. And alone. Summer season *boketto* moments can also occur during vacation in the company of others. Shared experiences. And that idea, vacation time, is next!

SUMMER

Vacation

Summer afternoon—summer afternoon; to me those have always been the two most beautiful words in the English language.
—Henry James

You are nearing the end of June, and your joy journey craves a boost. You can still feel the residue and impact of the previous season on your mind, body, and spirit. Rest, reminiscing, and *boketto* moments are essential letting-go moments, but now it is time to distance yourself from the previous school year and take a vacation! Maybe you are on vacation right now!

MY JOY

There are two highly effective ways to boost your mood and impact your joy this summer: (1) social connection and (2) time spent in nature.[122] The *social prescription* of a vacation is exactly what the doctor would order to give you the keys to walk through the joy door all summer long.

Social prescription, you ask? Yes!

There is a strong endorsement from the medical community that there are nonclinical steps you can take to improve your well-being. The practice, dubbed *social prescription*, includes doctors writing prescriptions for social activities to address feelings of isolation

Briefly describe your vacation plans for this summer.

_____
_____
_____
_____
_____
_____
_____
_____
_____
_____
_____
_____
_____
_____
_____
_____
_____
_____

and stress. Nature walks, arts and crafts workshops, concerts and museum exhibitions, community gardens, and other activities like vacations can bring a sense of meaning.[123]

So, yes, be intentional about going on that vacation and make sure summer afternoons are part of an experience that engages you, your family members, and your friends in the outdoors and all the gifts nature offers during the summer months.

∞

I have *the* picture.

We were hiking on a ridge, single file, in a fierce rainstorm, soaked and wet. Bent over against the wind, wondering what the heck we were doing out there. Our trekking poles were slipping out of our gloved hands, and we could barely see through the mist and rain. And it was cold. Maybe 40 degrees Fahrenheit.

It was my fault.

I had used my trail app and map to find a "fun" hike along the south end of Jökulsárlón—a glacial lagoon that is a part of the Vatnajökull National Park in Iceland. The lagoon is dotted with icebergs from the edge of the Vatnajökull glacier. The lagoon flows through a narrow gateway into the Atlantic Ocean; it was awe-inspiring, standing on the ridge and observing the flow of the icebergs for miles.

We had saved up for several years for this trip and talked about taking a vacation there often. And when we were ready, the circumstances of life caused a few more years of delay. Now we were there on vacation. Considering we are just normal humans that don't do a *lot* of hiking, the weather caught us a little off guard, and in the moment when the weather turned, all we wanted to do was get back to Thor (the name we had given our rental van).

Reminiscing about the moments right before the storm smacked us around, I remember the beauty surrounding us, the wonder and awe at the thunderous sounds of icebergs calving. The beauty of the place, the physicality and mental intensity required to overcome the challenge of the storm, and the comradery among the six of us.

Close friends, forever.

We each, of course, have our own unique interpretations and distinct memories of that moment of pure joy. The sheer magnificence and connection to something spiritual. Something far bigger than any one of us.

And, I have *the* picture.

It's the six of us and Thor. Thor is the only vehicle in sight. Other travelers had had the good sense to get out of the storm. But there we were, standing and sitting near the back end of Thor's open doors, soaking wet, cold, in the mist and the gray, satisfied smiles on our faces, shivering, and drinking Icelandic gin and tonics, with a wee bit of local ice secured from the glacier lake.

Exhausted *and* joyful.

It is rare that a vacation with friends or family can exceed your best hopes, yet our trip—with the off-the-grid quiet away from the noise of our phones and computers—was captured in that one simple picture. That picture made it to my "wall of memories" hall of fame.

I am a firm believer in the way certain people cross our life path, and how we each become better, stronger, and more courageous because of the crossing—arm in arm together—one moment at a time. One summer vacation at a time.

∞

Great summer vacations are whatever you want them to be. Planned or spur of the moment. Restful or active. Slow mornings or not. Sleepy afternoons or not.

For some of you, explorations of places unknown present your best summer memories. For others, it is repeatedly returning to a favorite place each summer with the comfort of exploring familiar grounds and places. Time alone or time with others. Close by or far away. Low cost or a special once-in-a-lifetime adventure. *Your choice.* Vacations are whatever you want to make of them. By balancing relaxation, personal growth, and enjoyable activities, you can have a fulfilling and rejuvenating summer vacation that prepares you for the new school year ahead.

── MY J O Y ──

Write about your wall-of-fame worthy best summer vacation ever! Tell your *who, what, when, and where* (*and maybe the why*) of your favorite vacation story.

_____
_____
_____
_____
_____

In life, we make decisions about the levels of friends we will let in. We use various adjectives to describe them. In my story, those friends are the best kind there are. They were, and are, more than best friends. They are confidants. And that level of friend is rare.

As we begin July, the family-friendship-joy connection is next.

SUMMER

Friendship

Friendship is born at that moment when one person says to another, "What? You too? I thought I was the only one."

–C. S. Lewis

It is the week of the Fourth of July! Time with friends and family. Like Thanksgiving, which ones will show up at your table for the July holiday party?

There have been many chapters in this book that encouraged you to find joy in moments alone, in silence, in nature . . . and more.

And yet, the joy you find in your daily moments alone, although necessary, will not be sufficient. Becoming a successful, high-character educator, family member, and human is never accomplished without the support of so many others in life.

This chapter and the three chapters that follow ask you to use the month of July to capture a clear picture of the mutually nourishing friendships in your life and show how to transition from one school year to the next armed with the joy benefits of those friendships.

MY JOY

There are several joy benefits we receive from the friendships we forge with family, colleagues, and

Intuitively, what are some of the joy benefits of your best friendships?

_____
_____
_____
_____
_____
_____
_____
_____
_____
_____
_____
_____
_____

neighbors. Research shows a strong connection between friendship and joy, highlighting how social connections can positively impact our mental health and overall well-being.[124]

- First, friendships stimulate our brains to release endorphins, which are natural mood boosters, helping reduce stress and enhance our feelings of joy. When we engage in social interactions, our brain also releases oxytocin, often referred to as the "love hormone," which strengthens bonds and creates a sense of trust and joy.[125]
- Second, close friends are a "must have," not merely a "nice to have." A close friend provides the emotional support essential for maintaining mental health. This support buffers against our daily stress and anxiety, leading to a more positive outlook on life. Friends offer companionship during tough times and celebrate successes, which contribute to a more joyful existence.[126]
- Third, studies using fMRI scans have indicated that when you are well-integrated into a social network, you have more synchronized brain activity, particularly in regions associated with emotions and empathy. This synchronization can enhance mutual understanding, compassion, and shared joy, making social interactions more fulfilling and enjoyable.[127]
- Finally, maintaining strong friendships has been linked to better physical health, including lowered blood pressure, reduced risk of depression, and longer lifespans. These health benefits contribute to overall well-being and joy.[128]

That is a lot of joy benefits. So, why is it so hard to do?

A big culprit is deciding who to be friends with, how many friendships to maintain, and what type of friendship to have with each person. Regardless of your friendship sources (family members, colleagues, community neighbors, or virtual or childhood friends), there are a few categories and levels of friendship to consider.

- *Acquaintances:* You are friendly, but the relationship is not deep (levels 1–2).
- *Casual friends:* You share common interests and group settings. The relationship is pleasant, but not too personal (levels 3–4).
- *Close friends:* You have stronger emotional bonds. You share personal experiences, offer mutual support, and spend significant time together (levels 5–6).
- *Best friends:* You share a deep, trusting relationship. Frequent communication, unconditional support, sharing life's ups

and downs. You call or meet up anytime when they ask you to (levels 7–8).
- *Confidants:* You share your most private thoughts and feelings. You carefully guard each other's deepest thoughts and wounds. You drop everything, anytime and anywhere, to be fully present when an emergency or crisis arises (levels 9–10).

I arrived at my fourth job as an educator (Stevenson HSD 125) in suburban Chicago at age 35. I was the newly minted director of mathematics and science. I was to lead fifty-four staff members, of which only a few were younger than me. I was a bit brash and perhaps a bit overconfident about how fast we could change our culture.

I also made a crucial leadership mistake. In my passion to get our faculty and staff to move the needle of student achievement forward as soon as possible, I failed to recognize the value of their past effort and actions to support current student performance. My ego was palpable, as I unintentionally signaled it was a new day and the present starts now—on my leadership watch, so to speak.

At that very moment, no one from that original staff viewed me as a friend. Not even levels 1-2. This would be something I would have to earn. By October, I had a few acquaintances. Some staff members were friendly, if a bit wary.

In late August, it was inadvertently announced to my staff by the building principal that I would be gone for a few days to receive an award from the White House. That award came with a stipend for the school, but I chose to donate the award to my former school, the place where the award had been earned the year before.

Initially, many of my staff were disappointed with me. Why did I not tell them about the award? Why were they not receiving the stipend, which could have helped with major computer, calculator, and hardware purchases? For my part, since I did not yet know them on friendship levels 3-4, I was just trying to lay low and not make a big deal about it. Yet my silence seemed to have made it worse.

And then, the day before I was to leave, Don (mathematics veteran) and Jim (science veteran) asked to see me in my office. They each told me in so many words how proud they were of me and wanted me to know I just needed to be patient and more transparent, as so many of my expectations for performance were new and happening quickly. They mentioned the award would bring positive attention to the school and to *find joy* in the three-day experience. Because of that moment of grace toward me, I was determined to intentionally develop a stronger emotional bond with them and take action to get to know Don, Jim, and their families better.

Fast-forward fifteen years. I was leaving my school-site job to become the district superintendent. Don and Jim had since passed away. Both had become *close* friends. I gave eulogies at both funerals at their families' requests. I had been to their homes in times of crisis. The staff that remained from that time fifteen years prior threw a "going to the district office and leaving us" party for me. They had become my friends and I theirs. Mostly casual, several close friends, and a few confidants. How blessed was I?

We had built our professional learning community progress on the back of those friendships.

Use the MY Joy space provided to list the names of friends that fall under each category, and then decide if you need to take actions to add, subtract, or move anyone into a different category.

MY JOY

Complete the table by listing the names of family members, professional friends, and community friends in the far-left column. Are you surprised by the sheer number of names? How many levels 7-8 or 9-10 friendships can you realistically maintain this coming school year?

Category

Acquaintances (levels 1-2):
___

Casual friends (levels 3-4):
___

Close friends (levels 5-6):
___

Best friends (levels 7-8):
___

Confidants (levels 9-10):
___

Those friends at the *confidant* level are hard to find and nurture, yet they are out there. There is another kind of friend, maybe someone at levels 11–12. A *naz* friend. Next!

SUMMER

Naz

Wherever you go, go with all your heart.
—Confucius

It's July, and I am wondering who a *naz* person in your life might be. You need them. You need their reassurance.

Naz? Yes, *naz* (pronounced *nahz*, with a soft *a*).

Naz is an Urdu word. A noun. A *naz* person loves you unconditionally. *Naz* persons convey admiration for your elegance, grace, and the way you exhibit confidence and charm. *Naz* persons are positive and highlight your endearing and admirable qualities. Your *naz* person recognizes and appreciates your worth and dignity and helps you feel valued and competent.[129]

Sounds good, right?

Your *naz* person always believes in you and puts a certain spring in your step. A smile on your face.

MY JOY

∞

When I met him, he was everything I was aspiring to be as a teacher. He was funny, wise, engaging, confident,

Do you have a *naz* person in your life? Name them! Write about them!

_____
_____
_____
_____
_____
_____
_____
_____
_____
_____
_____
_____
_____
_____
_____
_____

a good dancer, president of our state organization, and students loved being in the classes he taught. Everyone wanted to hang out with him. He was beloved because he recognized the worth and dignity in everyone he met. He was *naz* personified.

Eventually, he would become my *naz* person.

He was thirteen years older than me. I was in my seventh school season of teaching, twenty-nine years old, when we first met. We lived in separate towns and taught in separate schools about forty-five minutes away from each other. In one of those rare occurrences that might happen once in your life, if you are fortunate, we became instant and steadfast friends. And that friendship served us through remarkably rough, as well as genuinely great, moments of life.

He was charming in a good way, adding a light-hearted and joyful dimension to our daily interactions. He brought a sense of playfulness into everyday life, often making the more mundane tasks enjoyable and filled with spontaneous joy. During our early years of working together, he gifted me a sense of self-respect and confidence that lead to greater joy and satisfaction in my daily life, as it helped me feel valued and more competent, especially during that early stage of my career.

He taught me how to be mindful of my actions, words, and presence. He reminded me that as my career grew, I needed to be careful about my messages, as others were listening to me now, following closely to what I had to say. I needed to be sure research supported my beliefs. He taught me to embrace a greater appreciation of the present, fostering a sense of contentment and joy despite the struggles sometimes swirling around my everyday life.

In the beginning, he was the leader between the two of us. Mentor and mentee. Over time, we became more like equal *naz* persons and partners, supporting one another to become the best versions of ourselves. We immersed ourselves in life, love, sports, music, family, and faith together. We traveled the United States for almost two decades, attempting to entertain educators with our special brand of fun and humor. We spoke with honest yet funny takes on the rigor and hope of educating students well. We did our best to model the authentic teaching of effective collaboration with others.

Eventually, partially due to our age differences, our career pathways diverged. His career and family life were slowing down, and mine were taking off. Our friendship was thick, but our roles were changing. I was becoming more the mentor and he the mentee. And yet, he was so strong in who he was, so mature and confident, he relentlessly and unconditionally cheered on all my victories and remained fully present for all my failures and defeats too.

He demonstrated an unconditional love and support for me that was, in hindsight, both rare and deeply moving.

And then, one day we were walking along a beach together after a long day of summer work. Our walks were one of the ways we tried to maintain daily balance. We walked almost three miles with no words spoken. We had become comfortable with the silence between us. Finally, he broke the silence and said, "I can't remember things." More silence for a while. And then I eventually asked, "What do you need me to do, and how do you need me to be?" My *naz* person needed me to turn the tables and now love him unconditionally, no matter how hard the disease would hit him. No matter how much emotional pain would exist for us, as the bright light of his mind slowly faded away.

And so, I did.

It's been several years since that terrible memory disease destroyed this incredible human being. I miss him fiercely. I had no idea how much I needed a *naz* person like him in my life until he was no longer there.

Sometimes, in the quiet hours of the morning, I allow tears to flow. I thank God for the joy of his life and presence, not just for me but for all the others who benefited from his *nazness* (it's not a word, but I wanted to make it one). What a gift to experience another human like that, just one time in your life. The sheer and pure joy of it still overwhelms me. The memories linger inside my grateful heart.

Becoming a *naz* person for others supports your joy journey. *Naz* people develop a positive self-acceptance, grace, and elegance that radiate outward, influencing how you perceive and interact with the world, providing a sense of belonging and identity, and enhancing their joy journey and yours. So, take time this summer to determine who your *naz* person is and thank them. Ask yourself, "Who needs me to be a *naz* person for them?" Be intentional. Go for it. Be there for them in the school year ahead! Or maybe for a lifetime.

MY JOY

Naz persons bring joy by acting with unconditional love and support for the growth of another person. In this space, write about a friend or colleague who acts as a *naz* person in your life. The person who cheers you on from the balcony!

Now think about how you might serve as a *naz* person for someone in your life during the next school season that awaits you.

During the next school year, your *naz* person will cheer your efforts to stretch yourself into new learning beyond the norm. Let them know you have chosen them for that role. The idea of *stretching*, as part of our ongoing educational life, is next.

SUMMER

Stretch

If you know something's going to work, it's not worth working on. It requires no courage. It requires no faith. It requires no skin in the game. Whether you're a spy or a teacher or a spouse or a painter.

—Eliot Peper

Here we go! Quick question. Answer it using the MY Joy space provided.

MY J O Y

Many of you who are reading this book are most likely in pursuit of some aspects of the PLC at Work life. This choice means a life in pursuit of forever improving. Improvement in your knowledge and skills, subject-matter content skills, relational intelligence, communication skills, shared leadership skills, instructional skills, assessment skills, technology skills, and more.

This means you seek to stretch your knowledge and skills from previous school years. The summer season, then—during your time away from the noise of the daily grind—also presents an opportunity to spark creativity into the various areas of your work life as you stretch outside your comfort zone (but not so far that

Briefly reflect on the past school year. How did you *stretch* to improve above and beyond the expected norms for your work life?

_____
_____
_____
_____
_____
_____
_____
_____
_____
_____
_____
_____

you break), and then meet the challenges presented by the upcoming school year head-on.

The question is: *What voices should you listen to when deciding what to stretch for and how far to stretch forward?* This is where your *naz* person or a best friend can be a great sounding board. You need a trusted voice whose only agenda is driven by cheering on your personal growth and well-being.

This leads to a joy hack to consider this summer: *Don't listen to what others think about you.* Especially those voices that don't really matter or don't really know you. Those voices will fail to bring you joy.

For your energy and attention to go into mastering your personal and professional game, you need to measure yourself against the one person that matters most—*you* and *your* own expectations, not the expectations others are imposing on you.

Your *naz* person knows this.

When I was deciding whether to go back to graduate school (a stretch goal for me), there were competing voices screaming at me—*yes, no, don't go, go.* My *naz* person merely asked me a question, "Do you believe you have enough mathematics knowledge to become a great high school math teacher?" My answer was *no*. And so, I left my job, went back to school, got an advanced degree in mathematics, taught classes at the university for a year, and *then* went back to teaching high school students, well-armed to do the heavy lifting required.

When I was asked to author my first mathematics textbook (another stretch goal), I worried about what others would think of me if my attempts to write failed. Or worse, if the books were used by teachers and then heavily criticized as poor writing and teaching.

My *naz* person asked me, "What is more important? Paying attention to the needs of others or worrying about what they think of you?" He was right, of course. The former is what my teaching life was all about. The latter was, at best, self-destructive. If I worried about failure or what others thought of me, I would never have had the courage to stretch out and try.

He also said, "I know you can do this. Go for it!" *Ah, the gift of confidence.*

A third time, he showed up for one of our beach walks—when we could find a beach, that is. The stretch decision in front of me was to become superintendent of my district or not. It would be a lot of new and rigorous responsibilities. Voices again were loud. *Don't do it; do it. You will be miserable; you will love it. People will hate you* (yes, they used the word *hate*); *people will think you're crazy.*

The voices, the doubts.

My *naz* person, wise as always, said, "Stop worrying about what *they* think." Essentially, he was saying the doubters don't know you. Stop wasting your time on the voices of people who just want to tear you down. If you have a heart attack (which I did), they are not the people coming to visit you. Don't waste your time on them. And again, he reminded me I would be great at the job. Just stay true to the vision and values for building a great place for adults and students to come to work, teach, and learn.

A few months later, we had our other walk on the beach, which I mentioned in the previous chapter, *Naz* (page 197). Now, it was my turn to assure him he had the strength and the courage to stretch and grow in this moment of his life.

I did not tell him that I wasn't sure I had the courage required.

Use self-reflection or perhaps reflect with a person you really trust regarding ideas for *stretching* as you plan for the school year ahead. The following are some ideas for stretching *during* the summer season.

- *Find a mentor or become a mentor* to another educator, fostering a mutually beneficial learning relationship.
- *Join or form a collaborative team* with other educators either at your school or outside your school. Share ideas, resources, and strategies for effective teaching. Connect through social media, online forums, and professional organizations to exchange ideas and resources.
- *Learn about and experiment with new educational technologies and AI tools* that can enhance your teaching, engage your students, help tweak elements of your curriculum, and create and develop digital lesson plans, instructional videos, or other digital tools to place in digital unit-by-unit folders to use in your classroom during the year.

The beginning of the new school year looms ahead. Use this time to self-reflect on improved knowledge and skills that will stretch you for the new fall school season ahead.

Remember, not *one* of us can rest on our old knowledge. Learning is a process of continuous improvement and is a reality of the profession we have chosen. Create your stretch plan *now*.

MY JOY

Write about your intentional stretch goals and plans for the upcoming school season. Consider connecting your stretch expectations to data you have collected from the previous school year.

_____
_____
_____
_____
_____
_____
_____
_____
_____
_____
_____
_____
_____
_____
_____
_____
_____
_____
_____
_____
_____
_____
_____
_____

Don't forget to ask your *naz* person for feedback and assurance—this voice is worth listening to. And speaking of your *naz* person, don't forget to show them some gratitude as the end of July approaches. This is the time and place to do so.

SUMMER

Gratitude

I want you to know joy, so we practice gratitude. I want you to feel joy, so we will learn how to be vulnerable.

—Brené Brown

Imagine I told you there is something that creates new connections in the bliss center of your brain, reduces your fear and anxiety by regulating stress hormones, enhances dopamine and serotonin release, and fosters new neural connections that help you think more positively.[130]

This *something* will also lead to increased daily joy *and* decreased symptoms of anxiety and depression with no side effects for you. And it is free. No financial cost, for life.[131]

I suspect, like me, you would want to know what this *something* is. I also suspect you know the answer based on the chapter title.

Gratitude.

Gratitude? Yes. Fascinating. Easy to *say*. Harder to *do*.

Gratitude: At the heart of how we live with a spirit of joy.

Gratitude: Feeds into our joy manuscript.

Gratitude: The *if* to the *then* of joy.

Gratitude: Reverses our priorities to appreciate the persons and events we *do* have in life.

Gratitude: For the shallow and the deep.

Gratitude: Dices up exclusion and feeds belonging.

Gratitude: Cascades toward you when you reach for it.

Write about your gratitude for this summer season of rest. Remember, *gratitude is an acknowledgment that there are persons, circumstances, and events that your life would not be the same without.*

_____
_____
_____
_____
_____
_____
_____
_____
_____
_____
_____
_____
_____
_____
_____
_____
_____
_____
_____

Gratitude: Starts with a daily *awareness* of others.

Gratitude: Ends with a daily *acknowledgment* of others.

Gratitude: Recognition that your life would not be the same without the persons and events driving along your personal and professional pathway.

MY JOY

He had a ninetieth birthday party in the basement of a local church. I flew 1,781 miles and drove another 72 miles to be there. I was a little late, wanting to stay in the background. I did not know many of his family members, and I would not recognize many of his colleagues. They were much older than when I last remembered or saw them.

He had a way of showing up for me repeatedly throughout my life. It was the least I could do to come see him. I parked in the church parking lot and drew a deep breath. I wasn't sure quite what to expect. It had been a while since we had been together. Geographical distance made email our primary method of correspondence.

I was not very good at this. I didn't quite know what to say or who to give the gift and card to. Small talk. About what? I felt oddly out of place. I had been away from this geographical area for the past seventeen years. Yet, I felt a twinge of homesickness as I walked into the church.

And then it washed over me. The nostalgia of church. It was just like the churches where I had sung with my father more than fifty years prior. Memories flooded in. The birthday party was down the stairs in the church basement. I headed to a first-floor restroom and splashed water on my face. Somehow, the simplicity of the bricks and mortar, this holy place, felt so much like home. A kind of comfort so unique to a God I so desperately seek.

I gathered myself and headed down the stairs. I ran into two friends from the past. Good, kind, and caring friends whose distance held them at arm's length, but time didn't.

We laughed, shared, and hugged. I told them I was writing this book. And like true *close* friends, they cheered on my effort. I could feel their kindness, and I was grateful for it.

I headed down the stairs, thinking I would say hi to his daughter, drop off the gift, and sneak out. It was crowded. There he was, seated at a round table, holding court. He had aged. We all do and will. He wasn't as mobile as his former farmer and teacher self once was. His wit, though, was as sharp as ever.

"Kanold, what the hell are you doing here?" was his way of telling me he was glad to see me. And that he loved me.

I didn't linger. There were many others ready to celebrate his remarkable and wonderful life well lived thus far. I went back upstairs after saying a few proper goodbyes. The sanctuary was down a hallway. I walked that way and sat down in an empty pew. The sun reflected and shone through the stained-glass windows. Gratitude for my teacher and friend, for the place I was sitting, and for my sensitivity to it all oozed out of my soul.

My ninetieth-birthday friend had been part of our *four amigos* team. He had created it. We met every year for almost twenty years. He and I were the only two left. We were the only *naz* persons still standing from our small support group.

It all started when he was my honors geometry teacher in high school. You just never know *your* reach.

Use the following list to help you practice daily gratitude as this month ends. The practice of gratitude is centered within a daily awareness and acknowledgment of events, places, or persons that bring meaning to your life. This summer, before the stress of the new school year starts, you should act on advice from one of the reviewers of this book, Leanne Olinger—an educator just like you. She suggests the following *daily gratitude* process:[132]

1. Sit in the morning silence for a few minutes.
2. Send out a prayer of gratitude or affirmation (verbally or written).
3. Say or write one positive affirmation for the day ahead.
4. Name one person you need to demonstrate gratitude toward today (awareness).
5. Then *acknowledge* that person!

The following is a gratitude starter list. Write about and show gratitude for the persons, places, and events in your life.

- *Persons:* Friends, family members, and colleagues
- *Places:* Observations of what you hear, smell, taste, touch, and see
- *Events:* Activities such as vacations, singing and dancing, book clubs, celebrations, achievements, birthdays, graduations, sports, arts, concerts, and more

MY JOY

Try the *daily gratitude* challenge! Fifteen minutes! Use the space provided, or try it on your own, using the prompts.

Sit in the morning silence for a few minutes. Write down when and where.

___

___

Send out a prayer (or a thought) of gratitude or affirmation verbally or written. Remember, focus on persons, places, or events in your life.

___

___

Say or write one positive affirmation for the day ahead. Think of persons and events.

___

___

Name one person you need to demonstrate gratitude toward today (awareness). Write their name and what you would like to say to them.

___

___

Acknowledge that person! Write about an experience when you demonstrated gratitude toward someone.

___

___

Gratitude consistently connects and reconnects us to our greater purpose. That *deep* topic is next!

SUMMER

Purpose

There is no greater joy than knowing you are fulfilling your purpose in life.

—Oprah Winfrey

A cursory search through Amazon on any given day yields more than sixty books on the topic of purpose. That is a lot of purpose and a lot of advice.

I know some of you are quietly grumbling a little bit. *It's summertime. Do we really need to discuss the deep concept of purpose? In four pages, no less? The two-month rest has felt so good.*

I know. Yet, I have waited forty-eight chapters to finally discuss the purpose-joy connection with you. As our summer season nears its end and we are more relaxed and less stressed, a new school year awaits. This *is* the perfect time for the discussion.

Soon enough, you will be buried by the daily details of duties and actions. Your life will start racing along at a pretty good clip, *again*. A *purpose* refresh is needed now to sustain your joy and well-being in the upcoming school year.

Quick question to get started!

MY JOY

How would you describe the difference between a *relevant* life and a *meaningful* life?

_____
_____
_____
_____
_____
_____
_____
_____
_____
_____
_____
_____
_____
_____

A *relevant life* connects purpose to the story arc of your life. *Why* is this your story?

Where have you been (you just finished an entire year of your career a few months ago)?

Where are you today (getting ready to transition to a new school year soon)?

Where will you be in the future?

How will your past and current actions launch you into the school season waiting for you, peeking around the corner?

Comedian Michael Jr. gets it. If you listen to him closely, he challenges us to understand how a relevant life connects us to our purpose. He states, "When you know your why, your what has more impact because you are walking in and toward your purpose."[133]

Ahh, part of purpose is about knowing and staying *connected* to your *why*—to your day-in, day-out; month-in, month-out; season-in, season-out; school-year-in, and school-year-out professional and personal story arc. Your professional *why*. *Why* pursue teaching and leading others? Because deep in the recesses of your brain, there is no other joy story for you. Despite how the costs sometimes outweigh the benefits, it is your identity. It is what your life has been designed for. Intentionally or not, you could not have chosen a different story arc.

A *meaningful life*, on the other hand, connects purpose (significance) to our relationships.[134] And, as mentioned in Fall, Chapter 8: Relationships (page 35), striving for experiences and achievements *with others* is our long-term joy goal.[135]

According to the World Health Organization (WHO), your mental wellness is a "state of mental well-being that enables people to cope with the stresses of life, realize their abilities, learn well and work well, and contribute to their *community* [emphasis added]."[136]

Focus your eyes on the very last word: *community*. Relationships are power sources for meaning-making and joy in our professional lives.[137] Our purpose, one that is personally meaningful, is to make a positive impact on the lives of others—our family, friends, students, colleagues, and neighbors. How great is that!

Joy will find you if you just look for it.

Those words were spoken to me by my *naz* friend during the summer season of one of the darker times in my life. The new school year was about to begin, and I was not mentally or emotionally prepared for the journey. It was one of those moments in life when the purpose light that usually shone brightly inside of me felt faint and dim.

How was I to bring joy to my students and colleagues when I felt so joyless? Meaningless. Purposeless. His conversation with me that day—to start looking for joy, choosing joy, acknowledging joy, finding simple joy, creating joy—struck a nerve. He brought me out of my self-pity slump. How would I respond?

Curating joy means to select (the best or most appropriate) joy journey stories, especially for presentation, distribution, or publication.[138] And that is exactly what my friend placed in front of me that day. He challenged me to write, change, and own my future story arc at a Harry Caray's restaurant in Chicago during lunch, and eventually, through dinner.

He spoke that day of an uncensored version of who I was, reminding me of my impact on others. This *naz* person made me laugh and cry, taught me to hope and pray, helped me to seek good, do good, and be kind forever. And long before brain research affirmed it, he knew these choices, if I would make them part of my story arc, would allow joy to show up on my doorstep once again.

And he was right, of course. I entered that new school season with renewed understanding that my personal and professional life had purpose. Built on knowing my daily *why* and building into positive and successful relationships. The exact gift our profession provides.

A new school season was about to begin. And my *naz* friend reminded me, joy is easier to choose when our purpose is relevant, meaningful, and crystal clear. No matter the pain. No matter the circumstances. Thank goodness I could declare, "I am a teacher."

Think of the school year ahead. Now imagine it is late May of that year. Your new-school-year story arc has ended. What will be the story you hope to write?

MY JOY

This is your future story arc. On the left side, write about your *why*, your relevance as an educator in the story arc of your life. On the right side, write about relationships with your students or colleagues and how they create meaning for you.

Why You Are an Educator	The Meaning of Your Relationships

It's anticipation time again. You are ready. You have rested, renewed, refreshed, and rechecked your purpose. Only one thing left to do. *Resfeber*. And that is next!

SUMMER

Resfeber

If you do not actively choose a better way, then society, culture, and the general inertia of life will push you into a worse way. The default is distraction, not improvement.

— James Clear

It's almost go time.

You can sense it . . . smell it, as you get ready to walk back into the school building. The new school year is about to begin. Another cycle, a one-year tour, begins once again.

The season of rest is almost over.

You are a full year older and wiser. You are prepared, yet wary. The known and unknown stare straight at you. You are ready to leave the season of rest, right? *Maybe*, you think. Once again, you will create new beginnings and dive headfirst into your chosen profession. There will be a familiar rhythm. It feels comforting to see your colleagues and friends and meet new students despite the hectic pace that awaits.

As you anticipate the start of the school year, you could be experiencing something called *resfeber* (pronounced *RACE-fay-ber*), a Swedish word. A noun loosely meaning "the restless beat of your traveler's heart before the journey begins."[139]

MY JOY

What aspect of the new school year and fall season ahead most excites you?

_____
_____
_____
_____
_____
_____
_____
_____
_____
_____
_____
_____
_____
_____
_____

Indeed, a new journey in your professional story arc is about to begin!

There is or will be a mixture of anxiety and anticipation as you transfer from the summer season and into the new school year. You start counting down the days and the hours. Your brain and your heart know you are going on another long journey. It is a marathon and not a sprint. *Stay measured and pace yourself,* you think. So, you pick up your school backpack, set out your clothes and shoes, and go boldly into the adventure of a new school year. An adventure most assuredly filled with the unexpected.

Resfeber is the perfect word to describe how I am feeling as I write this final story for you. My educator story arc, unlike other stories in this book, is being written in *this* moment. Literally, as I type these words for you.

I chose *resfeber* for this chapter title because it provides insight into many of the joy pursuits in this book. I like the concept and meaning it has. We have each experienced travel journeys. We have also been on emotional-wellness journeys, personal growth journeys, professional growth journeys, and relationship journeys. Heart and soul journeys.

And now, *joy journeys*.

I chose *resfeber* because I am coming close to the end of my journey with you. Here's the thing. As I write this final story, I am feeling a bit overwhelmed by the irony. My joy as an educator has always been in the knowing, the anticipation, the challenge, the anxiety, and the stirring of riding into *another* school year with the challenge of another fall, winter, and spring season ahead. I am alive with *resfeber*; *the restless beat of my heart before the new school year begins.*

I have had fifty-three summer endings followed by new fall beginnings. Another school year filled with so much hope. So many possibilities. Fifty-three seasons of teaching feels selfish (did I stay in it too long?), with a twinge of wanting just one more.

Unlike many of my contemporaries, I am leaving on my own terms. Something that did not happen for them. I am deeply grateful for every one of those fifty-three seasons and the thousands of colleagues and students that got in the boat and rowed with me.

This time, I will not be starting over with you other than through this book, if you choose to read it and write your joy manuscript once again. I will miss the work fiercely. Yet, as we discussed in Fall, Chapter 10: Time (page 43), time waits for no one. And my time is here. To head off to a different rhythm and drumbeat of life.

I am not worried, though. I know you are tough. I know you have the courage it will take. And I know if you start to waver and wobble, you can always pick up this book again, perhaps with a *naz* friend, a mentee, or a mentor. Give each other the gift of choosing joy.

As I leave you to continue educating the next generation of children well, I want to share a poem with you, "The Joy of My Day."[140]

During the writing of this book, my wife and I expanded our friendship with community friends. We moved our vulnerability to friendship level 5, maybe level 6 at times. Pam is an artisan and artist. She paints, she draws, she writes. She's shy in a way. She's gifted.

I reached out and asked her to share some of her poems with me. I told her I wanted to include one of them in my new book on joy. It took great courage for her to share them with me; treat this poem with the kindness it deserves.

Do me a favor before you read her poem. Listen to your favorite music, which places you in the right frame of mind to embrace the *new school season* ahead of you. I am listening to the song "Sunshine" by pianist Jim Brickman as I choose her poem and write these lines.[141] Sometimes, life pulls our work together in mysterious and thoughtful ways.

I hope her poem creates a moment of joy for you as you begin the privilege of a new school year beginning. The fresh start of a new year, a new fall season, a new day. A new day? Yes, the joy of a new day and a new season ahead, indeed. May it be joyful.

The Joy of My Day

The clouds are now white
The sun's reflection has brought them to full life
They are spread out and cotton
Puffy and white
A Joy in my day.
Sitting in my bed watching the color of the sky and the clouds completely change, nature is art
the best there is, the best there will ever be.
This time is preparing me
Preparing me for creating
Painting
This is a joy of my day.
The joy of my day

Source: © 2023 by Pamela Snell. Used with permission.

MY JOY

Take a moment to reflect on Pam's poem. What part connected with you?

Write and then share about your preparation for designing and creating new experiences toward joy in the upcoming school year.

We are near the end. Time is up. You might still be wondering about my tattoo—my *why not* discussion in Spring, Chapter 8: *Zotheka* (page 151). That answer is the title of this chapter, *Resfeber*. A simple reminder of the restless beat of my heart for the work I love so much. May you also connect to the simple yet deep joy in the privilege of the new season ahead.

One last conversation with you awaits. And that, my friends, is the truth.

SUMMER

To get the full value of joy, you must have someone to divide it with.

—Mark Twain

Dear reader: I am writing this final chapter in part 4 different from the others. It is written as a dialogue between me and you as we approach the end of summer. Your voice is in italics.

Truth

What have you learned about joy along the way?

You mean me?

Yes, you read the book. Any thoughts?

Joy is hard.

Ha! So true. What else?

Joy is worth it. I am responsible for my own joy.

Meaning?

I own and create my own joy manuscript.

Care to share any insights?

Hmm. I am more than what I do. What I have. What others think of me.

True. And?

I can't buy joy! It's homegrown. Only I can create it. Cultivate it. Joy is not some fluke that just happens.

Agreed. Joy occurs when you and I pause our inner voice long enough to stop and simply appreciate a beautiful sunset, for example. Right?

Right, like when I am fully present despite all those darn plates I keep spinning. Joy feels like a gift I can grab right out of the blue. Anything else you would like to share with me before I go?

Yes.

What is it?

Regardless of the turmoil ahead, remember to sit in the stillness, don't be afraid of the storms, and radiate infinite confidence, kindness, compassion, and joy.

That will be my eulogy virtues I leave behind, right?

Now you're cooking!

Are we done here?

Almost. The great terms of a joy-filled life are *faith*, *hope*, *love*, *joy*, and *peace*.

These are not *just* feelings. They are conditions involving every part of your physical life, placed within the social context in which you live and work.

Woah. That seems a bit deep.

It is. These tenets displace the bitter and angry feelings that can characterize our teaching life. *Faith, hope, love, joy*, and *peace*—let's call them the "big five"—are inseparable from one another and reciprocally support each other.

Wow! Thanks.

No worries. You got this. Don't listen to the joy vampires. Carve your own path. Plot your own joy. Make it an ongoing part of your life story.

The students are waiting. The new colleagues are waiting.

They are waiting for me?

Yes. They are waiting for the joy you will find in them and bring to them.

Thanks for bringing me along for the joyride of this book. Get it, joy ride?

Ha! You are welcome. Without you, it would have been a lonely ride for me.

I was glad to be here. It got me through a tough year.

Joy is inside you. Inside your crazy heart. *You* got this! Know this. I will miss you, but I am so joyful for you. Always. I promise.

Summer:
A Season to Rejuvenate
Your Conclusions

During this summer season of rest, which of the joy actions in Summer chapters 1–11 most resonated with your current personal and professional joy journey? And thanks for making it through the book!

MY JOY ♥

In reflection, what are three to five brief takeaways about growing strong during the summer season as you transition into the beginning of a new school year and fall season that looms just ahead?

_____
_____
_____
_____
_____
_____
_____
_____

You can check out my video as I provide conclusions and insight from Part 4: Summer—A Season to Rejuvenate. Thanks for joining the summer journey with me. Keep a reminder of your purpose and your friendships close as the new school year begins.

Afterword

I'm filled with gratitude and inspiration as I sit down to reflect on everything Tim has shared with us in *JOY!* If there's one thing I've learned from reading this book and knowing Tim as I do, it's that joy is so much more than just a fleeting feeling. It's a way of life—a compass guiding us back to what truly matters, and, perhaps most importantly, a practice that we can all cultivate, regardless of our circumstances.

Let's be real. Working in education is tough. We know that the demands placed on our hearts, minds, and bodies can be overwhelming. We're tasked with inspiring young minds, supporting our colleagues, and meeting ever-growing expectations, all while trying to maintain some sense of balance and sanity in our own lives. It's easy to feel depleted—like joy is a luxury that only a few people can afford. But Tim has given us the beautiful reminder that joy isn't just a nice-to-have; it's essential to our well-being, our resilience, and our ability to keep doing this incredible work we've been called to do.

As educators, we are wired to serve, to give, to pour out our energy for the sake of others. But what happens when we give so much that there's nothing left for ourselves? This is where Tim's message really hits home. He challenges us to see joy not as an afterthought or a reward we give ourselves after we've accomplished everything on our to-do list, but as a foundation—a place to start *and* a place to land. When we choose joy for ourselves, we create the kind of energy that can light up an entire room, school, and community.

One of the most powerful ideas Tim shares in this book is that joy is a choice. It's not something that just happens to us; it's something we can intentionally cultivate. Yes, life will still throw us curveballs; yes, there will be days when finding joy feels like searching for a needle in a haystack. But Tim's wisdom reminds us that joy is still there, even in the struggle, even in the messiness of real life. It's in the laughter shared with a colleague after a long day, the smile from a student who finally "gets it," and the quiet moments of reflection when we recognize how far we've come.

Joy is not something we experience in isolation. It's magnified when we share it with others, when we lift each other up, and when we celebrate each other's victories—no matter how big or small. As educators, we have this unique opportunity to create cultures of joy within our schools; we set the tone and lead by example. We get to be joy-bringers, joy-builders, and joy-sustainers for ourselves and those we serve. (I am so lucky to be in community with Tim; he is an absolute joy-bringer in my life.)

As you close this book, let Tim's words remind you that you are worthy of joy—not someday, not when you've checked off everything on your list, but right here, right now. Let his wisdom inspire you to take small, intentional steps toward living a more joyful life, knowing that each step you take has the power to transform not only your own heart but also the hearts of those around you.

Joy is not a destination; it's a journey. It's a practice that we return to, day after day, even when life gets complicated and messy. It's about choosing to see the good, even amid challenges, and allowing that choice to shape our experiences. Tim has given us the road map, but the journey is ours to take. And I believe with all my heart that if we commit to this journey, if we prioritize joy in our lives, we can change the world—one classroom, one student, one colleague, one heart at a time.

So, let's make a promise to ourselves, right here, right now: to seek joy, to nurture it, to share it, and to live it with our whole hearts. Let's be the ones who lead with love, who inspire with hope, and who shine with joy. Because when we do that, we create a legacy that will last far beyond our time. We create a life worth celebrating, filled with purpose, passion, and unending joy.

Tina H. Boogren

Acknowledgments

In Spring, Chapter 10: *Meraki,* I shared this Greek word that roughly translates to the pouring of yourself wholeheartedly into something with soul, creativity, and love. If you are giving your best throughout the year, the product (your masterpiece for the school year) is the result of your thousands of day-to-day interactions, decisions, connections, revisions, interventions, collaborations, discussions, creations, and more. And it is *your* story.

This book is such a product, representing three years' worth of a joy journey and effort with so many incredible people who helped me along the way.

There was the season of new beginnings as I pitched the idea of a book dedicated to living a life of joy to Solution Tree Press leaders and friends Douglas Rife, Sarah Payne-Mills, Kendra Slayton, Todd Brakke, and Jeff Jones. Their 100 percent support meant everything to me. Thank you for your continued trust.

During that season of new beginnings, I interviewed friends, family members, and colleagues inside and outside of our wonderful profession. These meetings were sometimes over Zoom or in person, one on one or in groups; in a noisy bar or quiet café; or in a classroom or on a nature walk. Everyone, and I mean *everyone*, gave generously of their time and talent to help me better understand what an educators' joy journey, well lived, felt like for them.

In my three filled-to-the-brim journals of notes and research for this book, there were more than 160 of you who gave me a small piece of your time and wisdom. Although too numerous for me to mention here, please know I am so grateful for your voices and for briefly coming along with me during the early part of this joy journey.

During the season of heavy lifting (the actual writing of the book), the idea of fifty chapters initially seemed a bit absurd until I shared some of my ideas for the seasons and chapters with people I trust—colleagues Bob Eaker, Tina Boogren, Mike Mattos, Janel Keating, Anthony Muhammad, Regina Owens, Luiz Cruz, and Bill Ferriter. You are role models and leaders of leaders—colleagues in the deep work of our PLC life. You know what it means to live a daily life with joy. My deep thanks to each of you.

The heavy lifting of writing occurs when no one is really watching. During the hours of research and discovery through the creative process for writing this book, I had doubts about everything: the sequence of chapters and topics, the tone, the viability of the research, and, most importantly, the stories I chose to better connect with you, the reader.

My wife, Susan—who walks the joy journey with me and provides me the peace, space, and place to write—was often the sounding board I needed. I cannot ever thank her enough. There was the night, too, when we sat around a kitchen table in Bend, Oregon, with our friends Kevin and Angela Stroh. They gave me the grace to listen and be interested as I worked on rough drafts and read some chapters to them for feedback. Thank you for your interest in this project as I was writing it. Your positive response encouraged my belief that the rough manuscript was ready for the reviewers.

Writing is, in a way, like teaching. The work is creative, yet sometimes can feel isolating and lonely. And then along comes incredible collaborators to give the manuscript depth, meaning, and a richness far beyond my own wisdom. Teammates Mona Toncheff, Erin Lehmann, Dan Cohan, and Georgina Rivera—you are my heroes. Thank you for giving me your time, words, ideas, feedback, and critical yet encouraging direction throughout the entire writing project! And for being *in* the joy journey with me. Your many suggestions and revisions reside in the pages of this book.

During the season of finishing well, my focus and intensity for the project sometimes lagged. Yet many colleagues came through to help me finish the manuscript for this book. A big shout-out and thank-you to reviewers Jeanne Spiller, Aaron Hansen, Heather Friziellie, Doug Fonda, Bill Barnes, Brandon Jones, Regina Owens, Jaclyn Kanold, Adrienne Turner, Leanne Olinger, Anisa Baker-Busby, Joshua Ray, Jasmine Kullar, Jill Lizier, Jack Baldermann, Claudia Wheatley, Pamela Snell, and Brian Buckhalter. You are exemplars of the *meraki* the rest of us should follow. I am the beneficiary of your friendship, kindness, and wisdom!

And then, as an author, there is the season of rest (sort of). You turn in the reviewed manuscript to the publisher. The season of heavy lifting is over. And yet, the cycle of new beginnings, heavy lifting, and finishing well is just beginning for the editors. Their efforts to collaborate with me, through to the end of the finished and more polished product, were incredible.

My deepest thanks to Christine Hood. As the lead editor on *HEART!*, *SOUL!*, and now *JOY!*, I will always be grateful for her wisdom, guidance, and ability to see what I cannot, and the investment of her time and talent into this joy project. Laurel Hecker, Amy Rubenstein, Jessi Finn, Laura Cox, Sarah Ludwig, Elijah Oates, Madison Chartier, Hilary Goff, and especially Rian Anderson—you are the steady, behind-the-scenes forces that brought light to this project. Thank you, once again, for helping me to finish well!

My thanks to each of you, the readers. You are the "now what?" that sustained me through the writing process. You are, for me, what brings meaning to the words, ideas, and hope that emanates from pursuing the choice of joy in your journey. I often imagined you reading the words and wondering how you might be responding. You, and the challenging yet worthwhile "seasons" that are ahead of you, are what sustained me on the days I really didn't feel like finishing. You, and all that you give every day to find joy in your work life, are why I started this project in the first place and gave you the best I had along the way, right through to the end. May your heartwarming life story as an educator become a *story of joy* for you and all those who benefit from your incredible life!

You might ask, "Where did you draw your inspiration from for a book such as *JOY!*?" That answer is simple: my daily life with my "FamBam," as our text chain is called. I have saved hundreds of texts from my family encouraging me during the writing of this book, asking me questions about progress, and genuinely wanting to know how it was coming along.

In one way or another, their story is intricately linked with mine and mine with theirs. I wouldn't have it any other way. Adam, Anna, Jess, Tim, Jaclyn, and Susan—may you know and feel the acknowledging joy you have given to my life. And, perhaps, the joy I have given to yours.

And finally, there is my 99-year-old aunt Dottie. Her life story, her heart, soul, and joy journey, will forever be intricately linked with mine.

We are *ubuntu*.

I am what I am because of who we all are, indeed.

Notes

Foreword

1 Kanold, T. D. (2017). *HEART! Fully forming your professional life as a teacher and leader.* Bloomington, IN: Solution Tree Press.

2 Kanold, T. D. (2021). *SOUL! Fulfilling the promise of your professional life as a teacher and leader.* Bloomington, IN: Solution Tree Press.

3 Will, M. (2022, April 14). *Teacher job satisfaction hits an all-time low.* Accessed at www.edweek.org/teaching-learning/teacher-job-satisfaction-hits-an-all-time-low/2022/04 on December 12, 2024.

4 Sparks, S. D. (2022, July 7). *Teacher and student absenteeism is getting worse.* Accessed at www.edweek.org/leadership/teacher-and-student-absenteeism-is-getting-worse/2022/07 on December 12, 2024.

Introduction

5 Collier, S. (2022, October 17). *How can you find joy (or at least peace) during difficult times?* Accessed at www.health.harvard.edu/blog/how-can-you-find-joy-or-at-least-peace-during-difficult-times-202210062826 on September 26, 2024.

6 Newman, K. M. (2020, February 18). *How much of your happiness is under your control?* Accessed at https://greatergood.berkeley.edu/article/item/how_much_of_your_happiness_is_under_your_control on June 19, 2024.

Part 1: Fall—A Season to Renew

7 G. Rivera, personal communication, April 27, 2024.

Chapter 1

8 Sheldon, K. M., & Lyubomirsky, S. (2012). The challenge of staying happier: Testing the Hedonic Adaptation Prevention model. *Personality and Social Psychology Bulletin, 38*(5), 670–680.

9 Ibid.

10 Bandura, A. (2008). An agentic perspective on positive psychology. In S. J. Lopez (Ed.), *Positive psychology: Exploring the best in people* (Vol. 1, pp. 167–196). Westport, CT: Praeger.

Chapter 3

11 Simple. (n.d.). In *The Britannica Dictionary*. Accessed at www.britannica.com/dictionary/simple on June 1, 2024.

12 Keng, S.-L., Smoski, M. J., & Robins, C. J. (2011). Effects of mindfulness on psychological health: A review of empirical studies. *Clinical Psychology Review, 31*(6), 1041–1056.

Chapter 4

13 Kanold, T. D., & Boogren, T. H. (2022). *Educator wellness: A guide for sustaining physical, mental, emotional, and social well-being*. Bloomington, IN: Solution Tree Press.

14 Ibid, p. 54.

15 Alderman, L. (2016, November 9). *Breathe. Exhale. Repeat: The benefits of controlled breathing*. Accessed at www.nytimes.com/2016/11/09/well/mind/breathe-exhale-repeat-the-benefits-of-controlled-breathing.html on September 18, 2021.

16 Balban, M. Y., Neri, E., Kogon, M. M., Weed, L., Nouriani, B., Jo, B., et al. (2023). Brief structured respiration practices enhance mood and reduce physiological arousal. *Cell Reports Medicine, 4*(1), Article 100895.

17 Ibid.

18 Seppälä, E. (2023, January 5). *For better well-being, just breathe*. Accessed at https://time.com/6244576/deep-breathing-better-well-being on June 26, 2024.

19 Ibid.

20 Ibid.

Chapter 5

21 Williams, F. (2017). *The nature fix: Why nature makes us happier, healthier, and more creative*. New York: Norton.

Chapter 6

22 Jacca-RouteNote. (2024, January 15). *How many songs on Spotify have less than 1000 plays* [Blog post]. Accessed at https://routenote.com/blog/how-many-songs-on-spotify-have-less-than-1000-plays on September 18, 2024.

23 Rand, P. M. (Host). (2023, June 29). How your brain benefits from music, with Larry Sherman [Audio podcast episode]. In *Big Brains*. Accessed at https://news.uchicago.edu/how-your-brain-benefits-music on June 26, 2024; Sherman, L. S., & Plies, D. (2023). *Every brain needs music: The neuroscience of making and listening to music*. New York: Columbia University Press.

24 Ibid; Ibid.

25 Ibid; Ibid.

26 Fauré, G. (1946). *Requiem in D minor, Op. 48 for four-part chorus of mixed voices with soprano and baritone soli* [Musical score]. New York: Schirmer.

Chapter 7

27 Yearning. (n.d.). In *Merriam-Webster's online dictionary.* Accessed at www.merriam-webster.com/dictionary/yearning on June 1, 2024.

28 Lieberman, D. Z., & Long, M. E. (2018). *The molecule of more: How a single chemical in your brain drives love, sex, and creativity—and will determine the fate of the human race.* Dallas, TX: BenBella Books.

29 Ibid.

30 Ibid.

Chapter 8

31 Wilkinson, S. T. (2024). *Purpose: What evolution and human nature imply about the meaning of our existence.* New York: Pegasus Books.

32 Danvers, A. F., Efinger, L. D., Mehl, M. R., Helm, P. J., Raison, C. L., Polsinelli, A. J., et al. (2023). Loneliness and time alone in everyday life: A descriptive-exploratory study of subjective and objective social isolation. *Journal of Research in Personality, 107.* https://doi.org/10.1016/j.jrp.2023.104426

33 Wilkinson, S. T. (2024). *Purpose: What evolution and human nature imply about the meaning of our existence.* New York: Pegasus Books.

34 Seligman, M. E. P. (2011). *Flourish: A visionary new understanding of happiness and well-being.* New York: Free Press.

35 DuFour, R., & Eaker, R. (1998). *Professional Learning Communities at Work: Best practices for enhancing student achievement.* Bloomington, IN: Solution Tree Press.

Chapter 9

36 Sharot, T., & Sunstein, C. R. (2024). *Look again: The power of noticing what was always there.* New York: One Signal, p. 2.

Chapter 10

37 Fung, B. J., Sutlief, E., & Hussain Shuler, M. G. (2021). Dopamine and the interdependency of time perception and reward. *Neuroscience and Biobehavioral Reviews, 125,* 380–391.

Chapter 11

38 Surprise. (n.d.). In *Merriam-Webster's online dictionary.* Accessed at www.merriam-webster.com/dictionary/surprise on June 26, 2024.

39 Guthridge, L. (2024, January 23). *Want to improve? Rewire your brain's neural pathways.* Accessed at www.forbes.com/sites/forbescoachescouncil/2024/01/23/want-to-improve-rewire-your-brains-neural-pathways on June 1, 2024.

40 Medina, J. (2014). *Brain rules: 12 principles for surviving and thriving at work, home, and school* (Updated and expanded ed.). Seattle, WA: Pear Press.

Chapter 12

41 Perseverance. (n.d.). In *Merriam-Webster's online dictionary*. Accessed at www.merriam-webster.com/dictionary/perseverance on April 16, 2024.

42 Seery, M. D., Holman, E. A., & Silver, R. C. (2010). Whatever does not kill us: Cumulative lifetime adversity, vulnerability, and resilience. *Journal of Personality and Social Psychology, 99*(6), 1025–1041. https://doi.org/10.1037/a0021344

43 Ibid.

44 McGonigal, K. (2020, January 6). *Five surprising ways exercise changes your brain.* Accessed at https://greatergood.berkeley.edu/article/item/five_surprising_ways_exercise_changes_your_brain on June 1, 2024.

Chapter 13

45 Hugo, V. (1887). *Les misérables* (Vol. 4). London: Routledge.

Part 2: Winter—A Season to Be Resolute

Chapter 1

46 Fleming, J., & Ledogar, R. J. (2008). Resilience, an evolving concept: A review of literature relevant to aboriginal research. *Pimatisiwin, 6*(2), 7–23.

47 Fredrickson, B. L. (2004). The broaden-and-build theory of positive emotions. *Philosophical Transactions of the Royal Society B: Biological Sciences, 359*(1449), 1367–1378. https://doi.org/10.1098/rstb.2004.1512

48 Sharot, T., & Sunstein, C. R. (2024). *Look again: The power of noticing what was always there.* New York: One Signal, p. 2.

Chapter 2

49 Newman, K. M. (2020, February 18). *How much of your happiness is under your control?* Accessed at https://greatergood.berkeley.edu/article/item/how_much_of_your_happiness_is_under_your_control on June 19, 2024.

50 Cleveland Clinic. (2022, March 23). *Dopamine.* Accessed at https://my.clevelandclinic.org/health/articles/22581-dopamine on June 1, 2024.

Chapter 4

51 Kanold, T. D. (2017). *HEART! Fully forming your professional life as a teacher and leader.* Bloomington, IN: Solution Tree Press.

52 Clear, J. (2018). *Atomic habits: Tiny changes, remarkable results—An easy and proven way to build good habits and break bad ones.* New York: Avery.

53 Ibid.

Chapter 5

54 Insufferable. (n.d.). In *Merriam-Webster's online dictionary*. Accessed at www.merriam-webster.com/dictionary/insufferable on March 24, 2024.

55 National Institute of Mental Health. (2023). *Seasonal affective disorder.* Accessed at www.nimh.nih.gov/health/publications/seasonal-affective-disorder on June 1, 2024.

56 Huddleston, T., Jr. (2024, March 15). *Success requires 'ample doses of pain,' billionaire Nvidia CEO tells Stanford students: 'I hope suffering happens to you.'* Accessed at www.cnbc.com/2024/03/15/nvidia-ceo-huang-at-stanford-pain-and-suffering-breeds-success.html on June 19, 2024.

57 Suffer. (n.d.). In *Merriam-Webster's online dictionary.* Accessed at www.merriam-webster.com/dictionary/suffer on March 24, 2024.

58 Trzeciak, S., & Mazzarelli, A. J. (2019). *Compassionomics: The revolutionary scientific evidence that caring makes a difference.* Pensacola, FL: Studer Group.

59 Germer, C. K., & Neff, K. D. (2013). Self-compassion in clinical practice. *Journal of Clinical Psychology, 69*(8), 856–867, p. 857.

60 Gibran, G. (1912). *The broken wings.* New York: Meraat-ul-Gharb Publishing, p. 96.

Chapter 6

61 Trzeciak, S., & Mazzarelli, A. J. (2019). *Compassionomics: The revolutionary scientific evidence that caring makes a difference.* Pensacola, FL: Studer Group.

62 Ibid.

63 Goleman, D. (1995). *Emotional intelligence: Why it can matter more than IQ.* New York: Bantam Books.

64 Kanold, T. D., & Boogren, T. H. (2022). *Educator wellness: A guide for sustaining physical, mental, emotional, and social well-being.* Bloomington, IN: Solution Tree Press.

Chapter 7

65 Worry. (n.d.). In *Merriam-Webster's online dictionary.* Accessed at www.merriam-webster.com/dictionary/worry on June 1, 2024.

66 Fear. (n.d.). In *Merriam-Webster's online dictionary.* Accessed at www.merriam-webster.com/dictionary/fear on June 14, 2024.

67 Taitz, J. L. (2024). *Stress resets: How to soothe your body and mind in minutes.* New York: Workman.

Chapter 8

68 Cozy. (n.d.). In *Merriam-Webster's online dictionary.* Accessed at www.merriam-webster.com/dictionary/cozy on June 14, 2024.

69 Sanders, E. F. (2014). *Lost in translation: An illustrated compendium of untranslatable words from around the world.* Berkeley, CA: Ten Speed Press, p. 11.

70 Sima, R. (2024, January 4). *Forget FOMO: Embrace JOMO to discover the joy of missing out.* Accessed at www.washingtonpost.com/wellness/2024/01/04/fomo-jomo-joy-missing-out on June 14, 2024.

Chapter 9

71 Kanold, T. D., & Boogren, T. H. (2022). *Educator wellness: A guide for sustaining physical, mental, emotional, and social well-being.* Bloomington, IN: Solution Tree Press.

72 Brackett, M. (2019). *Permission to feel: Unlocking the power of emotions to help our kids, ourselves, and our society thrive.* New York: Celadon Books.

Chapter 10

73 Danvers, A. F., Efinger, L. D., Mehl, M. R., Helm, P. J., Raison, C. L., Polsinelli, A. J., et al. (2023). Loneliness and time alone in everyday life: A descriptive-exploratory study of subjective and objective social isolation. *Journal of Research in Personality, 107.* https://doi.org/10.1016/j.jrp.2023.104426

74 Turkle, S. (2012, February). *Connected, but alone?* [Video file]. TED Conferences. Accessed at www.ted.com/talks/sherry_turkle_connected_but_alone? on June 10, 2024.

Chapter 11

75 Blanchflower, D. G., & Graham, C. L. (2022). *The mid-life dip in well-being: A critique. Social Indicators Research*, *161*(1), 287–344, p. 342.

76 Blanchflower, D. G., & Graham, C. L. (2022). *The mid-life dip in well-being: A critique. Social Indicators Research*, *161*(1), 287–344.

77 Ibid.

78 Ibid.

79 Rauch, J. (2018). *The happiness curve: Why life gets better after midlife.* New York: Bloomsbury, p. 69.

Chapter 13

80 Grant, A. (2007). *Mosaic: Pieces of my life so far.* New York: Flying Dolphin Press, p. 161.

Part 3: Spring—A Season to Show Resolve

Chapter 1

81 Cerretani, J. (2011, Summer). *The contagion of happiness: Harvard researchers are discovering how we can all get happy.* Accessed at https://magazine.hms.harvard.edu/articles/contagion-happiness on June 14, 2024.

Chapter 2

82 Kanold, T. D., & Boogren, T. H. (2022). *Educator wellness: A guide for sustaining physical, mental, emotional, and social well-being.* Bloomington, IN: Solution Tree Press.

83 Newman, K. M. (2024, March 21). *World happiness report isn't so happy for young Americans.* Accessed at https://greatergood.berkeley.edu/article/item/world_happiness_report_isnt_so_happy_for_young_americans on June 14, 2024.

84 Cerretani, J. (2011, Summer). *The contagion of happiness: Harvard researchers are discovering how we can all get happy.* Accessed at https://magazine.hms.harvard.edu/articles/contagion-happiness on June 14, 2024.

Chapter 3

85 Credibility. (n.d.). In *Merriam-Webster's online dictionary.* Accessed at www.merriam-webster.com/dictionary/credibility on April 27, 2024.

86 Amabile, T. M., & Kramer, S. J. (2011, May). *The power of small wins.* Accessed at https://hbr.org/2011/05/the-power-of-small-wins on June 14, 2024.

87 Norman, M. (2020, February 18). *What makes you credible? It's not what you (or they) think* [Blog post]. Accessed at www.mattnorman.com/what-makes-you-credible-its-not-what-you-or-they-think on June 14, 2024.

88 Neer, M. (2018, July 3). *EDI activates 18 of the top 30 influences on student achievement, as measured by Hattie* [Blog post]. Accessed at https://dataworks-ed.com/blog/2018/07/edi-hatties-visible-learning on June 14, 2024.

89 Enthusiasm. (n.d.). In *Merriam-Webster's online dictionary.* Accessed at www.merriam-webster.com/dictionary/enthusiasm on June 9, 2024.

Chapter 4

90 Wolsink, I., Den Hartog, D. D., Belschak, F. D., & Oosterwijk, S. (2019). Do you feel like being proactive today? Trait-proactivity moderates affective causes and consequences of proactive behavior. *PLoS One, 14*(8), Article e0220172.

91 Meylani, R. (2024). Exploring the link between mindset and neuroscience: Implications for personal development and cognitive functioning. *International Journal of Research and Analytical Reviews, 11*(1), 748–764.

92 Kun, A., & Gadanecz, P. (2022). Workplace happiness, well-being and their relationship with psychological capital: A study of Hungarian teachers. *Current Psychology, 41,* 185–199. https://doi.org/10.1007/s12144-019-00550-0

Chapter 5

93 Gallup. (n.d.). *State of the global workplace.* Accessed at www.gallup.com/workplace/349484/state-of-the-global-workplace.aspx on June 14, 2024.

94 Ibid.

Chapter 6

95 Siegle, S. (2023, August 17). *The art of kindness* [Blog post]. Accessed at www.mayoclinichealthsystem.org/hometown-health/speaking-of-health/the-art-of-kindness on June 14, 2024.

96 Alden, L. E., & Trew, J. L. (2013). If it makes you happy: Engaging in kind acts increases positive affect in socially anxious individuals. *Emotion, 13*(1), 64–75.

97 SSM Health. (2022, November 8). *The science behind kindness and how it's good for your health* [Blog post]. Accessed at www.ssmhealth.com/newsroom/blogs/ssm-health-matters/november-2022/the-science-behind-kindness on June 14, 2024.

98 Ibid.

99 Boothby, E. J., & Bohns, V. K. (2021). Why a simple act of kindness is not as simple as it seems: Underestimating the positive impact of our compliments on others. *Personality and Social Psychology Bulletin, 47*(5), 826–840.

Chapter 7

100 Regret. (n.d.). In *Merriam-Webster's online thesaurus.* Accessed at www.merriam-webster.com/thesaurus/regret on May 3, 2024.

101 Pink, D. H. (2022). *The power of regret: How looking backward moves us forward.* New York: Riverhead Books.

102 Ibid.

Chapter 8

103 Guthrie, S. (2024). *Mostly what God does: Reflections on seeking and finding his love everywhere.* Nashville, TN: W Publishing Group.

104 VandeHei, J. (2024). *Just the good stuff: No-BS secrets to success (no matter what life throws at you).* New York: Harmony Books.

Chapter 10

105 Sanders, E. F. (2014). *Lost in translation: An illustrated compendium of untranslatable words from around the world.* Berkeley, CA: Ten Speed Press.

Chapter 11

106 Valedictory. (n.d.). In *Merriam-Webster's online dictionary.* Accessed at www.merriam-webster.com/dictionary/valedictory on June 27, 2024.

107 Ibid.

108 Hansen, A. (2024). *Heroes within: A framework for empowering students to own their learning journeys.* Bloomington, IN: Solution Tree Press.

Chapter 12

109 Metz, T., & Gaie, J. B. R. (2010). The African ethic of *Ubuntu/Botho*: Implications for research on morality. *Journal of Moral Education, 39*(3), 273–290.

110 Ibid.

Part 4: Summer—A Season to Rejuvenate

Chapter 1

111 Pang, A. S.-K. (2016). *Rest: Why you get more done when you work less.* New York: Basic Books.

112 Ibid.

113 Grant, A. (2023). *Hidden potential: The science of achieving greater things.* New York: Viking.

114 Pang, A. S.-K. (2016). *Rest: Why you get more done when you work less.* New York: Basic Books.

115 Grant, A. (2023). *Hidden potential: The science of achieving greater things.* New York: Viking.

Chapter 2

116 Reminiscence. (n.d.). In *Merriam-Webster's online dictionary.* Accessed at www.merriam-webster.com/dictionary/reminiscence on June 2, 2024.

117 Speer, M. E., & Delgado, M. R. (2017). Reminiscing about positive memories buffers acute stress responses. *Nature Human Behaviour, 1*(5), Article 0093.

118 Heath, C., & Heath, D. (2017). *The power of moments: Why certain experiences have extraordinary impact.* New York: Simon & Schuster.

Chapter 3

119 Sanders, E. F. (2014). *Lost in translation: An illustrated compendium of untranslatable words from around the world.* Berkeley, CA: Ten Speed Press.

120 Sharot, T., & Sunstein, C. R. (2024). *Look again: The power of noticing what was always there.* New York: One Signal.

121 Ibid.

Chapter 4

122 Boodhoo, N. (Host). (2023, November 30). Laurie Santos: Finding connection in lonely times [Audio podcast episode]. In *1 Big Thing*. Accessed at www.axios.com/2023/11/30/laurie-santos-finding-connection-in-lonely-times on May 16, 2024; Robbins, J. (2020, January 9). *Ecopsychology: How immersion in nature benefits your health*. Accessed at https://e360.yale.edu/features/ecopsychology-how-immersion-in-nature-benefits-your-health on June 5, 2024.

123 Caron, C. (2024, April 25). *When the prescription is for a dance class, not a pill*. Accessed at www.nytimes.com/2024/04/17/well/mind/social-prescription-health-medication-art.html on June 28, 2024.

Chapter 5

124 Mineo, L. (2017, April 11). *Good genes are nice, but joy is better*. Accessed at https://news.harvard.edu/gazette/story/2017/04/over-nearly-80-years-harvard-study-has-been-showing-how-to-live-a-healthy-and-happy-life on June 27, 2024.

125 Mayo Clinic Staff. (2022, January 12). *Friendships: Enrich your life and improve your health*. Accessed at www.mayoclinic.org/healthy-lifestyle/adult-health/in-depth/friendships/art-20044860 on June 19, 2024.

126 Khan, H., Giurca, B. C., Sanderson, J., Dixon, M., Leitch, A., Cook, C., et al. (2023). *Social prescribing around the world: A world map of global developments in social prescribing across different health system contexts*. London: National Academy for Social Prescribing. Accessed at https://socialprescribingacademy.org.uk/media/4lbdy5ip/social-prescribing-around-the-world.pdf on June 27, 2024.

127 Fallon, N., Roberts, C., & Stancak, A. (2020). Shared and distinct functional networks for empathy and pain processing: A systematic review and meta-analysis of fMRI studies. *Social Cognitive and Affective Neuroscience, 15*(7), 709–723.

128 Mayo Clinic Staff. (2022, January 12). *Friendships: Enrich your life and improve your health*. Accessed at www.mayoclinic.org/healthy-lifestyle/adult-health/in-depth/friendships/art-20044860 on June 19, 2024.

Chapter 6

129 Sanders, E. F. (2014). *Lost in translation: An illustrated compendium of untranslatable words from around the world*. Berkeley, CA: Ten Speed Press.

Chapter 8

130 Zahn, R., Garrido, G., Moll, J., & Grafman, J. (2014). Individual differences in posterior cortical volume correlate with proneness to pride and gratitude. *Social Cognitive and Affective Neuroscience, 9*(11), 1676–1683; Zahn, R., Moll, J., Iyengar, V., Huey, E. D., Tierney, M., Krueger, F., et al. (2009). Social conceptual impairments in frontotemporal lobar degeneration with right anterior temporal hypometabolism. *Brain: A Journal of Neurology, 132*(3), 604–616.

131 Bolier, L., Haverman, M., Westerhof, G. J., Riper, H., Smit, F., & Bohlmeijer, E. (2013). Positive psychology interventions: A meta-analysis of randomized controlled studies. *BMC Public Health, 13*(119).

132 L. Olinger, personal communication, May 16, 2024.

Chapter 9

133 Bayside Church. (2020, July 28). *Michael Jr. / Walking in your "WHY"* [Video file]. Accessed at www.youtube.com/watch?v=E2T7BacFpOo on June 19, 2024.

134 Meaningful. (n.d.). In *Merriam-Webster's online dictionary*. Accessed at www.merriam-webster.com/dictionary/meaningful on June 10, 2024.

135 Wilkinson, S. T. (2024). *Purpose: What evolution and human nature imply about the meaning of our existence.* New York: Pegasus Books.

136 World Health Organization. (2018). *Mental health: Strengthening our response.* Accessed at www.who.int/news-room/fact-sheets/detail/mental-health-strengthening-our-response on July 6, 2021.

137 Danvers, A. F., Efinger, L. D., Mehl, M. R., Helm, P. J., Raison, C. L., Polsinelli, A. J., et al. (2023). Loneliness and time alone in everyday life: A descriptive-exploratory study of subjective and objective social isolation. *Journal of Research in Personality, 107*. https://doi.org/10.1016/j.jrp.2023.104426

138 Curate. (n.d.). In *Merriam-Webster's online dictionary*. Accessed at www.merriam-webster.com/dictionary/curate on June 8, 2024.

Chapter 10

139 Sanders, E. F. (2014). *Lost in translation: An illustrated compendium of untranslatable words from around the world.* Berkeley, CA: Ten Speed Press.

140 P. Snell, personal communication, June 9, 2024.

141 Brickman, J. (2010). Sunshine [Song]. On *Home*. Somerset Entertainment, Ltd.

Index

A

acknowledging joy. *See also* joy
   finishing well and, 125–126
   in spring, 127–130
acquaintances, 194. *See also* relationships
administrative changes, 48
anxiety
   acts of kindness and, 143
      boketto and, 185
      box breathing and, 20
      nature and, 24
artisans, being artisans, 159–162
authenticity, xii

B

balance, 103–107
beginnings
   in fall, 7–10
      growing strong in a season of new beginnings, 5–6
best friends, 194–195. *See also* relationships
boketto, 3, 185–188
box breathing, 20, 101
brain chemistry
   gratitude and, 205
   joy and, 2, 69
   kindness and, 143
   music and, 28
   relationships and, 49, 194
   yearning and, 32, 33
breathe/breathing, 19–22, 101
building credibility, 126

C

casual friends, 194. *See also* relationships
celebrations, seeking celebrations, 65
chronic joy, 66–70. *See also* joy
classroom assignments, 51
close friends, 194. *See also* relationships
collaborative teams, 203

community. *See also* relationships
   joy and, 9, 38
   purpose and, 210
   ubuntu and, 167–170
commuovere
   graduation and, 122
   in spring, 155–158
   use of term, 3
comparison, 75–80
compassion, 87–90, 101
competence, 132
confidants, 195. *See also* relationships
counting, 101
coziness, 96–97
credibility, 126, 131–134

D

daily gratitude process, 207
daily rest breaks, 180
dopamine, 2, 28, 32, 33, 69, 143

E

emotional intelligence, 88
endorphins, 2, 143, 194
engagement, 139–142
enthusiasm and passion, 133
environments, classroom environments, 48

F

fall
   beginnings, 7–10
   breathe, 19–22
   growing strong in a season of new beginnings, 5–6
habituation, 39–42
hijacked, 47–50
   music, 27–30
   nature, 23–26
   perseverance, 51–54
   relationships, 35–38

remember, 11–14
simple joy, 15–18
Thanksgiving, 55–57
time, 43–46
yearning, 31–34
your conclusions, 59–60
family and friends breaks, 180. *See also* relationships
fear, 92
finishing well
    compliment cards and, 145
    growing strong in a season of, 121–122
    in spring, 123–126
friendship, 193–196. *See also* relationships
future success, preparing for, 126

G

gezellig
    balance and, 104, 106
    boketto and, 185
    credibility and, 133
    use of term, 3
    in winter, 95–98
goals, 31–34. *See also* yearning
gratitude, 164, 205–208

H

habit formation, 77–78
habituation, 65, 39–42
happiness
happiness curve, 109–110
happiness versus joy, xii, 1–2
hijacked/joy hijacking, 47–50

I

inaction regrets, 148–149. *See also* regrets
introduction, 1–4

J

joy
    about, 1–2
    acknowledging joy, 125–126, 127–130
    chronic joy, 66–70
    happiness versus joy, xii, 1–2
joy connections, 38
joy hijacking, 47–50
joy journeys, definition of, 1, 16, 21
    simple joy, 15–18
    use of term, xii
"Joy of My Day, The" (Snell), 215

K

kindness
    regrets and, 100
    reminiscing and, 183
    in spring, 143–146

M

making-the-time commitments, 44–46
meaningful lives, living, 210
mental well-being, 9, 17, 24, 46, 81, 210

mentors and mentorship, 203
meraki
    graduation and, 122
    in spring, 159–162
    use of term, 3
Michael Jr., 210
midlife, 109–112
mindfulness
    balance and, 106
    box breathing and, 20
    pausing and, 99, 100–101
    simple joy and, 17
    worry and practicing mindfulness, 93
mini-breaks, 41
moral character, 135–136
music, 27–30

N

nature, 23–26
naz, 3, 197–200

O

oxytocin, 2, 49, 194

P

pause, 98–102
performing character, 135–136
perseverance, 51–54
physical wellness, 9
possibilities/it is possible, 153–154.
    See also zotheka
preparation, 126, 135–138
purpose, 209–212

Q

QR codes, 4, 60, 120, 174, 220

R

reactive and responsive mindsets, 99
reflection, 113–116
regrets, 100, 147–150
relationships
    credibility and, 133
    in fall, 35–38
    family and friends breaks, 180
    impact of, 49
    purpose and, 210
    reminiscing and, 183
    seeking out joy, 65
    suffering and, 84–85
    ubuntu and, 167–170
    remember, 11–14
reminiscing, 181–184
resfeber, 3, 213–216
resilience, 64, 69
resolution/resolute persons
    growing strong in a season of heavy lifting, 61–62
    in winter, 63–66
rest
    growing strong in a season of, 175–176
    in summer, 177–180

S

screen-free me time, 106
self-awareness, 99, 104
self-care, 65, 154
self-challenge, 52
self-compassion, 52
self-efficacy, 52
Seppälä, E., 21
serotonin, 2, 143, 205
show/showing up, 117–118
silence, 71–74
simple joy, 15–18
Snell, P., 215
social awareness, 88
social prescription, 189
social wellness, 9
spring
   acknowledging joy, 127–130
   commuovere, 155–158
   credibility, 131–134
   engagement, 139–142
   finishing well, 123–126
   growing strong in a season of finishing well, 121–122
   kindness, 143–146
   meraki, 159–162
   preparation, 135–138
   regrets, 147–150
   ubuntu, 167–170
   valedictory, 163–166
   vanaprastha, 171–172
   your conclusions, 173–174
   zotheka, 151–154
stories, 155–158. *See also commuovere*
stress
   boketto and, 185
   box breathing and, 20
   habituation and, 65
   joy journey and, 1, 16, 21
   kindness and, 144
   nature and, 24
   positive reminiscence and, 182
   relationships and, 194
self-care and, 154
simple joy and, 17
   worry and, 92
stretching knowledge and skills, 201–204
student assignments, 47
student needs, 47
suffering, 81
summer
   boketto, 185–188
   friendship, 193–196
   gratitude, 205–208
   growing strong in a season of rest, 175–176
   naz, 197–200
   purpose, 209–212
   reminiscing, 181–184
   resfeber, 213–216
   rest, 177–180
stretching knowledge and skills, 201–204
   truth, 217–218
   vacation, 189–192
   your conclusions, 219–220
surprises and finding joy, 47–50

T

teams
   collaborative teams, 203
   remember, 11–14
technology, 203
temporary actions, 41
Thanksgiving, 55–57
time
   in fall, 43–46
   make-the-time commitments, 44–46
time-off breaks, 179
   work and time constraints, 48
truth, 217–218

U

ubuntu
   acknowledging joy and, 129
   graduation and, 122
   in spring, 167–170
use of term, 3

V

vacation, 189–192
valedictory, 163–166
vanaprastha, 171–172

W

winter
   balance, 103–107
   chronic joy, 66–70
   comparison, 75–80
   compassion, 87–90
   gezellig, 95–98
   growing strong in a season of heavy lifting, 61–62
   midlife, 109–112
   pause, 98–102
   reflection, 113–116
   resolution/resolute persons, 63–66
   show/showing up, 117–118
   silence, 71–74
   suffering, 81
worry, 91–94
   your conclusions, 119–120
World Health Organization (WHO), 210
worry, 91–94

Y

yearning, 31–34

Z

zotheka, 3, 151–154

Praise for

JOY!

Growing Strong Throughout Your Seasons of Life as a Teacher and Leader

"In *JOY! Growing Strong Through Your Season of Life as a Teacher and Leader*, author Timothy Kanold offers an eloquent and heartfelt invitation to educators and leaders to rediscover and sustain the joy that energizes their professional and personal lives. Building on the brilliance of *HEART!* and *SOUL!*, this book masterfully weaves the metaphor of the four seasons into a rich narrative that mirrors the rhythms of a school year. Through inspiring ideas, personal stories, and impactful strategies, Kanold encourages readers to keep joy at the heart of their work and lives. Whether you are beginning your journey or have navigated many seasons, the reflections prompt you to pause, reconnect with your purpose, and reimagine your joy journey. Both inspiring and practical, *JOY!* is an essential guide for anyone committed to truly thriving in education."

—**Georgina Rivera**
Principal, West Hartford Public Schools, Connecticut

"Timothy Kanold's *JOY!* is the perfect companion to his two previous highly popular books, *HEART!* and *SOUL!* Using the seasons of the year to frame the role joy plays in our lives, this book is more than inspiring—Each "season" provides encouragement and suggestions for seeking joy in our own lives, both personally and professionally. Like Kanold's previous books, readers are sure to find this latest book to be pure joy!"

—**Robert Eaker**
Professor Emeritus, Middle Tennessee State University

"*JOY!* inspires and transforms. It made me think, reflect, and consider joy in ways I never had before, encouraging me to find joy even in the simplest and most routine parts of life. I love how honest and real it is, framed with relatable stories that connect deeply to both the heart and mind. This book doesn't just describe joy; it shows how to embrace and sustain it through life's rhythms. Practical, heartfelt, and profoundly inspiring, it is a must-read for anyone seeking to nurture joy in their personal and professional journey."

—Jeanne Spiller
Solution Tree Associate

"*JOY!* is a remarkable book that captures the essence of embracing joy amidst life's complexities, especially in the field of education. Its seasonal framework provides a relatable and actionable pathway to sustained joy. The heartfelt and authentic stories offer humor, hope, and deep emotional resonance, such as the touching *Naz* chapter, which brought me to tears. Educators, often overwhelmed by expectations, will find this book particularly grounding with its practical strategies, relatable experiences, and reminders of the importance of reflection and relationships. Each chapter is perfectly sized to fit into a busy schedule, making it an ideal companion for those seeking joy amidst life's busyness. With refreshing candor and insightful perspectives, *JOY!* inspires readers to embrace the beauty of their current 'season' and discover enduring joy."

—Erin Lehmann, Assistant Professor
University of South Dakota

"In *JOY!*, author Timothy Kanold has written a concluding masterpiece to his educator empowerment and professional wellness series that includes *HEART!* and *SOUL! JOY!* builds off these great works but also stands alone as a guide for educators as they navigate the changing 'seasons' of the school year. Educators will find various themes, including connection, relationships, stories, purpose, reflection, vision and wellness. Through its insightful passages, stories, prompts and opportunities for reflection, *JOY!* will resonate with all educators and leaders. This book provides a unique literary experience, where the reader learns to cultivate joy in their personal and professional lives through a deep reflection of, and draft plan towards, their own joy journey."

—Daniel Cohen
Retired Chief of Schools, Jefferson County Public School District, Colorado

"*JOY!* is a beautifully crafted guide that blends heartfelt personal stories with research-based practices to support educators in nurturing their well-being. Organized by the seasons, this book offers a unique structure that mirrors the natural ebb and flow of the school year, making it easy to follow sequentially or dip into for inspiration as needed. Whether you're looking to reflect on renewal in spring, embrace growth in summer, navigate change in autumn, or find rest in winter, this book meets you where you are. Its balance of relatable anecdotes and practical strategies makes it an indispensable resource for educators seeking to thrive both personally and professionally."

—Scott Hagerman
Superintendent, Tanque Verde Unified School District, Arizona

Praise for JOY!

"Author Timothy Kanold continues the *HEART!* and *SOUL!* journey with his latest book, *JOY!* As I read the compelling stories and completed the MY Joy spaces throughout the book, I was continually reminded of how important it is to choose joy—not just for myself, but also for those I serve. Kanold's storytelling and emotional insights illustrate how to create and foster joy during each season of the school year and how to steer clear of joy vampires. This is a must-read on your joy journey!"

—Mona Toncheff
Author, Consultant, and Past President of the National Council of Supervisors of Mathematics

"*JOY!* is a delightful experience that will help any educator unlock the secrets to increased resilience and deeper levels of fulfillment. Timothy Kanold's wisdom unfolds through personal stories and intentional reflection. Each chapter culminates with an interactive exercise to set the reader on their path to sustain joy throughout the school seasons. Reading *JOY!* is like having a personal coach to help navigate educators' challenges to renew a sense of passion and purpose. I highly recommend binge-reading it first and then using it as a weekly reflection journal—a must-read for educator wellness and sustainability."

—Leanne Olinger
Instructional Coach, Springfield Middle School, Fort Mill, South Carolina

"*JOY!* guides the reader through a series of reflective exercises in pursuit of the simple joy that, when nurtured, can replace the relentless cacophony of distractions in our lives with a soothing soundtrack of centeredness. The book is written in such a way that it can be started on any page, depending on the season and the needs of the reader. *JOY!* is the perfect capstone to the *HEART!* and *SOUL!* collection."

—Bill Barnes
Superintendent, Howard County Public School System, Maryland

"As educators, it can be so easy to lose sight of the passion that first drew us to this work. That's why I was so moved by *JOY!* Author Timothy Kanold's unique approach to reigniting that spark offers inspiring stories and practical strategies to keep readers connected to what originally drew them to education. It reminded me of why I originally chose this profession and filled me with a renewed sense of purpose. This book is a must-read for every educator who wants to find renewed purpose and joy in their work!"

—Joshua Ray
Educational Consultant, Coach, Speaker, and Author

"Now more than ever, *JOY!* is a necessary text and must-read for all educators—each of us who has chosen the education profession. Author Timothy Kanold creates a neuroscience- and research-affirmed pathway to sustained joy throughout all seasons of one's life as an educator. The book highlights how joy can become an internal, intentional pursuit and weave its way through the tapestry of your daily life. Let's begin reading!"

—Janel Keating
Author and Educational Presenter

"Timothy Kanold's *JOY!* is a masterfully written accompaniment to his previous work in *HEART!* and *SOUL!* By combining a mix of personal stories from over fifty years as an educator with the neuroscience of wellness, Kanold offers educators tools to navigate the various seasons of each school year and professional career with dignity and fulfillment. In an era when educators are navigating unprecedented challenges, this book serves as a beacon of hope and inspiration. It reminds us that the work of teaching and leading is not just about standards and outcomes—it's about humanity, connection, and purpose—those things that bring us joy! Kanold's compassionate and authentic voice makes this book a must-read for anyone committed to the profession of education."

—Scott Harrison
Superintendent, White River School District, Washington

"Every educator should have a copy of Timothy Kanold's *JOY!* within reach as they navigate the complex, nuanced, and sometimes overwhelming seasons of their work. This inspiring book is filled with poignant storytelling, thoughtful reflection, and practical strategies that are all masterfully woven together to create an interactive guide that challenges and inspires educators to embrace the continuous journey of *choosing* a life filled with enduring purpose and most importantly, *joy*!"

—Paula Maeker
Author and Educational Consultant

"In *JOY!*, Timothy Kanold writes, 'Joy is an internal action, walking through life because of the good, and despite the difficult circumstances we live within.' I agree that the intentional internal act of choosing joy connects us and helps us cultivate a mindset of simple joy. I am deeply grateful as a person and professional that Kanold calls us back to finding meaning and purpose in the small ordinary aspects of our personal and professional lives. My heart is overjoyed with what is to come for our care as educators and our community as learners as we choose to grow in each season, inspiring all students and igniting a passion for teaching and leading once again."

—Regina Stephens Owens
Author and Educational Consultant

"In *JOY!*, Timothy Kanold writes with the warmth of a friend and the wisdom of a mentor, sharing compelling stories that pull you in and gently prompt simple, yet profound reflection. Clearly a reflection of his own joy, this timely book is an infectious read that guides us through rediscovering our purpose, balance, and the *joy* available inside each one of us!"

—Aaron Hansen
Author and Educational Consultant

Global PD teams
Collaborative Learning for School Improvement

Quality team learning **from** authors you trust

Global PD Teams is the first-ever **online professional development resource designed to support your entire faculty on your learning journey.** This convenient tool offers daily access to videos, mini-courses, eBooks, articles, and more packed with insights and research-backed strategies you can use immediately.

GET STARTED
SolutionTree.com/**GlobalPDTeams**
800.733.6786